HUMBLE HERO

Charles T. Joyner

outskirts
press

Outskirts Press, Inc.
http://www.outskirtspress.com

ISBN: 978-1-9772-0451-6

Library of Congress Control Number: 2018911659

PRINTED IN THE UNITED STATES OF AMERICA

Foreword

This is my father's story, Charles Robert Joyner. He was a humble hero who lived and survived a time of terrible war and economic depression. His is a story of a troubled childhood, love, unusual war experiences, and deep religious convictions. This account is drawn from his recordings, conversations, letters, and military records. He began life as an orphan, struggled through his teenage years as a ruffian, and matured to become a loyal husband, distinguished soldier, devout Catholic, and outstanding citizen.

He rarely discussed details of his young life or wartime experiences until he was an old man. When he agreed to tell his story, he insisted it should be used to help young family members understand the sacrifices he and his buddies made to secure their freedoms. He consistently credited his survival as a gift from God and not the result of luck or his own efforts.

In writing this memoir, I used his words and phrases extensively while placing chronological references to guide the reader. I inserted a handful of more descriptive words in some places, but based upon his telling and my research, the events described herein are all true. In my research, I was fortunate to hear first-person accounts from other Bataan Death March survivors and their descendants. I also read extensively about the war in the Philippines between 1941 and 1944, which verified the people, places, and dates referenced. While some of his language may be considered harsh or insensitive to some readers, it fairly reflects the emotions he experienced at the time about the horrific events he encountered and ultimately survived.

I wish to extend heartfelt thanks to my wife, Peggy, who endured, perhaps enjoyed, my periods of absence as I plodded along with this project. Thanks as well to my daughter, Charmaine, for her encouragement and to the Preston, Harris, Blair, Tebault, and Vaughn families, who encouraged me to press ahead despite my doubts and bouts of laziness. Thanks are also extended to cousin Michael Conrey for his inspirational comment that became the title, *Humble Hero*.

I dedicate this work to my late mother and father and the millions who perished, sacrificed, or survived the terrible war and economically harsh years of the 1940s. I am convinced their efforts and patriotism guaranteed America as a safer and better homeland for future generations.

Finally, I have arranged for a substantial portion of proceeds from this book be donated to reputable veteran organizations and charities.

Table of Contents

Early Years—Orphanages

Well, Tommy, here goes. I guess I'll start from the beginning. I was born in Portsmouth in 1918 and baptized a few months later at St. Paul's Church. I was the youngest of five children born to Annie May Culpepper and Lemuel Joyner. Mother died when I was a little squirt, and I don't remember much about her. Some say she died from Spanish flu or pneumonia. My mom was only twenty-nine when she passed. From old pictures she was a pretty lady, and my sisters inherited her good looks. Daddy wasn't around much because of his work and a beating that injured his brain. Mother's family, the Culpeppers, adopted me and my brothers.

One the earliest things I remember was a big wad of brown spit hitting me square in the face. It tasted and smelled awful and made me throw up. It was Grandma Lula's chewing tobacco. She loved the filthy stuff and spat it everywhere. One day my brothers, Willy and Elwood, and I were running around her home playing chase. She was sitting above us on the porch, chewing and rocking in her wicker chair. When we ran past her, she let go a big mouthful, and the goo came

1

flying and hit me. Covered in the slimy brown ooze, all the grown-ups and kids laughed like hell. My brothers laughed so hard they fell on the ground and rolled around like spinning tops.

Next earliest memory was when I was three or four years old. I remember sitting on a train squeezed between Willy and Elwood. Grandma had pinned tags on our coats and ordered us to not remove them until we got to Roanoke. It was a chilly morning, and big fat raindrops began splashing on the window. Inside the train it smelled like a mix of smoky oil and dust, but I was excited because it was my first train ride. I felt pretty special. The train jerked a few times and then slowly began to move away from the Portsmouth station. The wooden floors vibrated, and the big iron wheels screeched. Out the window I saw Grandma, Granddaddy, and my daddy standing in the rain waving. My father was holding Grandma's hand and looking away. But, as the train slowly moved, he finally looked at us and gave a little grin. A few minutes out of the station, the sound of rain ended, and tiny chips of ice and sleet began to softly pelt our window. I knew this was going to be an adventure and felt safe sitting between my big brothers. Willy was the oldest and always happy and laughing. He liked to play tricks and tickle and tease me. Elwood was the tallest and quiet, more serious than Willy. He had a good reputation as a fighter and was usually in charge. I was the smallest, and for some reason they nicknamed me Dinky and rarely addressed me as Charles.

Being a little kid, I had no idea why we were leaving home on a train so I asked Willy, and he revealed we were heading to St. Vincent's in Roanoke. It was a Catholic orphanage for boys. He explained that Grandma and Granddaddy already had too many kids and couldn't look after three extra boys and my two sisters. So the three of us were heading for an orphan home in Roanoke, and our sisters, Mary and Peggy, were going to St. Joseph's Villa in Richmond. Willy reminded me that when Daddy got severely beaten and robbed one night coming home from the Seaboard Shops, his brain got a little jumbled, which meant he lost part of his thinking and common sense. At the time, I didn't exactly know what that all meant. Our father was a small man and was always nice to us, but he only visited us at the Culpeppers' on Sunday for dinner. Additionally, Willy reminded me that when Mama died, the Culpeppers didn't think Daddy could properly raise five children, so they took us into their home. I didn't cry or feel bad about the situation but felt a little bad it might be a long time before I would see Daddy and my sisters again. I knew my brothers were my only family now and felt secure since they were older and bigger than me.

The train got colder as snow began blowing around outside. Our window got frosty, and the little potbelly stove in our car wasn't doing much to keep us warm. I huddled closer to Willy and Elwood to get warm and comfortable. At some of the little stations, I waved at the people waiting on the platforms. We passed little towns, farms, and homes with chimneys puffing white smoke. I remember wondering what the people in those houses were doing. I guessed the kids in those homes were watching our train and would envy my first train ride and upcoming adventures in Roanoke. After a few hours chugging along, hills replaced the flatland and everything outside became covered by a giant white blanket.

3

Elwood opened a brown bag nestled between his long legs and pulled out a bologna sandwich and a little apple for each of us. This was our lunch and dinner. Next thing I remember, Willy smacked me on the head and told me to wake up. It was now dark, the train had stopped, and we had reached Roanoke. I trudged off the train through deep fluffy snow following my brothers. Within minutes my feet and legs became wet and felt frozen. A big fat lady in a long black dress and white hat with floppy wings met us and ordered us to follow her. She rushed us along and used her long rosary beads, hanging from her waist, to smack my fanny a few times. We hustled into a waiting bus with a few other boys and lurched away from the train depot.

Our new home, St. Vincent's, was run by the Sisters of Charity. For the most part, they were good to us but always strict. Nobody was permitted to miss a bath, toothbrushing, or meal when the sisters were watching. However, when they weren't watching, we fought each other like hell. Punching and shoving was a favorite activity for the boys. Bloody noses, busted lips, and scratches were common. Although there were only thirty or forty boys, arguments over toys, one's place in the dinner line, or food portions led to skirmishes and fisticuffs. This was my first experience with serious fighting. Willy and Elwood had always teased me, but our wrestling and fighting was always in fun. Most of the boys at St. Vincent's were older and bigger than me so I got picked on a lot. Some of the boys were bullies, and everyone seemed intent to determine who the toughest guy was. This competition resulted in lots of shoving and punching whenever the nuns weren't watching. Right off the bat, since I was one of the smallest guys, everyone wanted to kick my butt and did. The first few weeks I got punched and pushed around plenty of times. My brothers never helped me and said I had to learn to fight back. They reminded me not to become a cry baby, so I began to fight back. At first it was slapping, and then I learned to clench my fists, punch, wrestle, twist arms, pull hair, gut punch, and do whatever I could to avoid a whipping. Even though I was scrawny, I quickly learned the only rule in fighting was to do your best to beat down the other guy. Before long, the other fellows knew I would fight back and didn't pick on me so much. Naturally there were a few tough boys I could never escape, and I expected and got a good thumping from them occasionally. The nuns rarely witnessed our fights, and when they saw the torn clothes or bruised and bloody results, we usually got a lecture. The sisters tried, always unsuccessfully, to determine the culprit, victim, and cause of the fisticuffs, but it was our unspoken code to never rat on each other.

We had chores between classes and church every day. Cleaning rooms, pulling weeds, doing laundry, helping in the kitchen, and other jobs were assigned daily. Classes were six days a week, and we were required to observe a study time every night. Once the nuns turned off the lights, talking was not allowed. However, we whispered jokes, giggled, and traded stories with each other until we got too loud and finally slept after several stern warnings. Something I didn't like was the small portions of food we got at every meal. While nobody starved, I remember being hungry all the time. The typical meal was juice or powdered milk, a piece of bread, a couple of little weenies or chunks of meat, and a few tiny potatoes. A popular variation was stews and soups with unknown meats and vegetables. If somebody didn't like or want their food, there were always takers for the leftovers. I don't think any food ever went to waste. We got a little more food on Sundays, holidays, or when someone from the parish donated something extra for the kitchen. I remember one time we got a big bag of candy, and the nuns gave everyone a few pieces. Man, oh man, I loved that candy, especially the chocolate pieces. Another time a man brought in several bushels of apples, and we ate apples for a few weeks. However, cakes, cookies, and candy were an exception to our normal food. Because they were older, Elwood and Willy got jobs in the kitchen and began to swipe food, which they shared with me.

We went to church every day, and goofing off at Mass, though normal, was strictly forbidden. A few times I got sent to the office for my irreverent behavior and got whacked pretty good with a wooden paddle by the head sister. Honestly though, there were times when somebody farted, made a goofy noise, or giggled, which caused me to laugh. One strict nun told me I was a bad boy, pinched my ear as she yanked me out of the pew, and told me I was going straight to hell if I didn't learn to behave in God's house. Well, she certainly scared me because I knew hell was an endless fire full of devils and monsters. It was a place I did not want to go, and after many scoldings I began to feel bad that I might end up in Satan's firepit. After every confession I vowed to do better at church, but I still messed up a lot. Sitting through a mass of Latin, jangling bells, kneeling, and standing was tough since I was never sure what it all meant.

Christmas was my favorite time. On the day Jesus was born, we got turkey, mashed potatoes, fresh vegetables, cranberry sauce, pie, cookies, and seconds. Some grown-ups visited their boys, but nobody ever visited us. We also received goody bags of hard candy, fruit, and cupcakes. Best of all, everybody got one new toy. It was usually a scooter, skates, or maybe a bicycle. An old man, dressed as Santa, visited Christmas morning after Mass, and dragged in sacks and boxes full of toys. Everybody got a present, even the bullies who I thought deserved lumps of coal. We helped decorate a big, fresh-cut evergreen, sang Christmas songs, and didn't have school for a few days. It was the best time of the year. Since each boy got only one toy, it had to last until the next Christmas. I got pretty good at fixing broken bikes and skates for the other boys and was eventually lent a few tools by the parish priest. In addition to repair jobs, I even jazzed up a few broken skates and scooters with painted flames and stars.

At St. Vincent's I first began to draw things. When the nuns weren't watching, I drew pictures of animals, airplanes, cartoon characters, and cars instead of doing my lessons. One of the sisters, I forget her name, told me I was pretty good at drawing and had talent. One Christmas, she gave me a box of colored chalk and allowed me to draw Santa, his sleigh, and reindeer on several of the blackboards. I got a kick out of doing this, and everyone said my pictures were good. The head nun allowed my pictures to remain on the blackboards well into January. Every year I attended St. Vincent's, I drew Thanksgiving and Christmas pictures on the blackboards and was pleased with my work and the praise it received.

After a couple of years there, Willy and Elwood were sent to another school. They told me they were going to St. Mary's

Industrial School in Baltimore. Initially I didn't like this because I was still a young fella and worried about being alone
without my big brothers. I was relieved when Elwood told
me I would be coming to St. Mary's when I turned ten. This
made me feel better and less worried about their impend-
ing absence. When they left, I became one of the older boys
in the place, and my last two years were good compared to
my first couple of years. I got better chores, could whip just
about anyone, and somehow learned to behave in church. I
also got on well with the nuns, and they granted me a few
extra privileges and larger dinner portions.

When I was ten, I got another train ride north to Baltimore.
I arrived at St. Mary's and was shocked. I couldn't believe
the huge school that Elwood told me was home to seven
hundred other boys. It was fenced in like a prison. This orphanage was run by a bunch of brothers, and believe me,
those guys were rough characters. Willy told me to be careful because this place was more a reform school than a
home for regular orphans. I soon noticed that a bunch of the
boys looked like gangsters or members of a dead-end gang.
Compared to St. Vincent's, this was a mean crowd of boys.
Within days it became obvious I was ranked probably 698th
of the seven hundred in the pecking order of fighters. To my
dismay, everyone was bigger and tougher than me. I got a lot
of whippings the first few months, and those damn brothers
always looked the other way unless somebody got cut up,
knocked out, or required an ambulance. I believe the brothers wanted us to fight or just didn't give a damn. It quickly
became apparent that I needed to be ever ready to mix it up
if I were to survive this joint. After my brothers gave me a
few a few tips on fighting, I gradually rose up in the ranks

of warriors. After I busted up a kid called Kissing Bug and a few others, I finally got a little respect. Nonetheless, I began not liking St. Mary's very much because it was like a jail full of thugs and run by a bunch of mean guys.

At St. Mary's we had daily classes, church, and never enough food at chow time. The St. Mary's toughs were downright dangerous compared to the boys at St. Vincent's. Naturally, we all had daily chores that included cleaning gutters and the mess hall, doing laundry room, painting, and gardening. Fortunately, the daily mass was a quick service. Few acted dopey during Mass, knowing well the vengeance of the brothers was swift and sometimes painful. However, I remember one crazy stunt. Boys from a neighboring dorm stole a bottle of altar wine from the sacristy and got drunk as skunks. By the next morning, they were sober. Nobody tattled on them, and it made the brothers mad as hell. An extra lock got installed on the sacristy door shortly after the wine heist. Since there were so many bad boys, someone was always pulling a stunt or starting a ruckus. Once in a while, police cars or ambulances came roaring through the opened front gates with their sirens blaring to carry someone off to jail or a hospital.

Willy got a job working in the kitchen, and since he was a smoker, we made a deal. In return for cigarette butts or any whole smokes I could swipe for him, he would sneak me extra food. At first I didn't do so well because Willy refused the tiny and nasty butts I delivered, but I learned to find fatter and longer cigarette butts, and my reward was a few extra treats.

I vividly remember one fall afternoon when, for no good reason, some punk walked up and without a warning gave me a bloody nose. Out of the blue he just walked up and sucker punched me in the face. Of course, no one saw his attack, and when I told a brother, he told me not to whine. After this dustup, I decided I was going to escape this awful place and go home. I was going to run away but realized I needed a plan. St. Mary's was partially surrounded by brick walls about six or eight feet high, along with wire fences making up most of the perimeter. Weeks earlier, while running around the grounds, I noticed some gaps under the rusty fences. The small spaces possibly dug out by dogs or other critters looked inviting, and I found one large gap that I thought I could squeeze under. One day after lunch, during our recess, I rushed to that fence, and when the bell rang for classes to resume, I made my move. The brothers usually lingered until the last boys entered the school, but I rushed to the hole that I figured was large enough for me to get through and decided it would be my escape route. As recess ended and everyone shuffled back into the school, and seeing only the backs of the brothers, I made my move. I crawled under the fence and ran like hell, never looking back till I was in downtown Baltimore. Nobody had seen me run away, and I blended in with the people walking along the sidewalk. It felt wonderful to be free of the bullies and brothers.

After aimlessly drifting around, I eventually went into a nickel-and-dime store. The customers and salesladies smiled; some even patted me on the head. I liked it when people were nice, and at only eleven I was still a skinny little guy, and many probably thought I was younger. It was early afternoon, and I guess they weren't used to seeing a little boy in the store at that time of day. A couple of old ladies told me I was cute little fellow and asked if I was lost or where my mama was. I gave them my best innocent smile and lied. I told them she was shopping in the lady's department. Several of them gave me a few pennies and told me to buy candy. Folks were busy getting things, and there were many good things to get. Soon I decided to get a few good things for myself. I drifted around, carefully pocketing what I wanted, and it was easy. First I filled one pocket with penny candy. In my other pocket, I stashed a little bag of peanuts, a small red ball, and a pack of Camels.

After goofing around in different stores and snitching a few more snacks, I walked along bouncing my red ball and chewing on some Mary Jane candies. We didn't wear uniforms at St. Mary's, and except for some dirt on my face and pants from crawling under the fence, I probably looked like any regular kid. I aimlessly drifted down one street and then another, and I think a few people thought I was a street kid and gave me a few coins. I lingered at a fruit stand, and the man there asked if I was hungry; when I nodded, he gave me a banana and an apple.

As the afternoon gave way to night, I still hadn't figured how I would get back to Portsmouth. I knew the train fare would be more than the few coins in my pocket. Hitchhiking was a possibility, but I didn't know which streets led home. It had been an exciting day and I was getting tired, so I started looking for a place to sleep. Walking a block away from a busy street of shops, I discovered a neighborhood of large fancy houses. Most of the places had light streaming out of the windows, but I found one that was dark inside and knew it might be the safest place to hide and rest. I found a hunk of cardboard and crawled under the front porch. After eating some candy, peanuts, and the banana, I curled up and thought about ways to get home. Half-asleep in pitch dark, I felt something rubbing my face. It was a big cat. It scared me awake so I smacked it, and the yellow puss ran off hissing.

Next morning I woke up, and it was chilly, but the sunlight squeezing through the floor cracks promised some warmth later in the day. As I quietly crawled from under the porch, leaving the cardboard in case I returned, I noticed two bottles of milk on the front porch. Quietly and out of sight, I watched and listened. After a few minutes, it seemed as though the people in the house might still be asleep, so I carefully crept up the steps, placed one bottle under my shirt, and descended the stairs to the sidewalk. After walking a few minutes and feeling safe, I popped the lid and sucked in the delicious milk. After wandering a few more blocks, I found a bakery and had enough change to buy a cinnamon bun, which I washed down with the rest of the milk.

On my second day of freedom, I kept trying to form a plan to get home. Walking along, I bounced my ball and chewed my remaining candies. It was fun looking in the shop windows at all the nice shoes, toys, and clothes. I wondered if I would ever be a rich kid or have any grown-ups buy me such nice things. On one street of fancy stores, I noticed many fine cars, well-dressed people, and even drivers in some of the cars. I knew these were rich people, and my eleven-year-old mind quickly realized the opportunities. First, I could get some more change if I stood around and looked pitiful. Next, I thought if I asked one of these rich people, someone might help me get back to Westhaven. The first part of my plan worked nicely, as ladies and even a few gents dropped coins into my cupped hands. Smiling and doing my best to look innocent, I pocketed a lot of jingling change. One old guy gave me a quarter dollar, which was a coin I had rarely seen. The second part of my scheme didn't work so well. When I asked people if they would take me to Portsmouth, some ignored me, some asked if I was lost, and others asked about my parents. However, the most worrisome comment from several people was for me to stay put, and they would call someone to help. I guessed they might be phoning the cops, so I quickly scooted away and moved deeper into the city toward some tall buildings. Along the way, I found a Boy Scout cap in the gutter, and since it wasn't wet or dirty, I put it on thinking this might change my appearance.

With the money people gave me, I bought a hot dog and Coca-Cola from a street vendor. I ducked into a drugstore and bought a big Tootsie Roll and chewed on it while I strolled along. With my belly full and being away from St. Mary's, I was having a swell time, but I kept wondering how the devil I would get back home. I didn't know a lot about geography but knew Portsmouth was a long way south of Baltimore. A train or bus ride would be the surest way, but tickets cost more money than the remaining change in my pocket. As I walked around some more, I noticed a boy about my age sweeping a store's floor and another riding a bicycle with a basket full of groceries. I thought maybe a little job could get me enough money to buy a ticket. I could certainly ride a bike, sweep or mop a floor, or stock shelves as well as any other kid, so I brushed the dust off my pants and shirt and asked about jobs in several shops and markets. No luck. The bosses either didn't have any work, or they asked where I lived and too many other questions. Disheartened, I used the last of my loose change to buy two bananas. I ate one right away and shoved the other into my pocket for later.

Stepping along the sidewalk of one street, which was very noisy with streetcars and automobiles, I remember coming upon a scruffy gray and white dog. It was sitting on the edge of the curb, wagging its tail and watching the traffic. I reached down to pet it, but it snarled and snapped at my hand. I slapped at the mutt and missed, and my red ball tumbled out of my pocket. The dog chased the ball, sniffed, and then chomped down on it. I yelled stop, but the dog looked back and raced down the sidewalk. I gave chase, and the little critter would momentarily stop, turn, and look back my way, wagging its tail, and then run farther away. After a while, I think the dog was playing. We ran many blocks, and I was having fun but getting a little winded. Finally, the dog stopped and dropped the ball. I cautiously approached and retrieved my ball. The dog's tail was wagging, and its eyes focused on me. I tried petting again, and this time it hopped around and seemed happy. Like me, I figured this little fella was getting by on the streets, and we became fast friends. I looked at the dog's private parts, realized it was a boy, and named him Lucky. I thought I was lucky to find a friend on the streets, and he was lucky to find me.

It was getting close to sunset, and I was tired and a little hungry, so I ate the other banana. I offered Lucky a little chunk, but he just licked it. As nighttime came, I passed a sign that said Patterson Park. It was a huge area of trees, lawns, and park benches bordered by city noise and lights. It had turned chilly, and I noticed some men stretched out on park benches and lying under the trees, so I thought this might be a good place to sleep. Lucky hopped up on the bench as I stretched out, and even though he was a little stinky, it was nice to have a buddy and not be alone. I thought about Willy and Elwood eating a hot meal and curling up under their blankets back at St, Mary's and wondered if I should return. After a while, an old guy came up to my bench and told me I would freeze if I didn't get covered up. He pointed to a pile of old newspapers by a trash can and said it would be warmer to sleep under a tree, using the newspapers and leaves as a blanket. There were many men in the park, and I guessed many were hobos. I thought it was funny that Lucky and I were now young bums. I found a soft spot under a tree. Using some newspapers and leaves, Lucky and I huddled together and got ourselves almost completely covered. For a while I listened to some of the nearby men snoring and muttering to themselves. One guy was even singing a song about his old mammy. Lying there, I also wondered what Granny and Grandpa Culpepper were doing, and if I got home, would they welcome me or ship me back to St. Mary's. Then I fell asleep.

In the morning things changed a lot. A little frosting of snow was on the ground. I was hungry and chilled to the bone. All the bums and Lucky were gone, and a huge policeman was standing over me. After gently poking me with his big black stick, he said, "Well, what ya up to, sonny?" He was grinning, so I didn't feel scared, but I didn't want any part of this cop. I jumped up and tried to run, but he grabbed me by the shoulder and held me in place. I knew I couldn't escape from this big man, so I just plopped down. He marched me a few blocks to a police station and had me sit on a long bench alongside a bunch of other guys who were probably crooks, drunks, or hobos. After a while, a cop came out and had me follow him into a room. "Hungry, kid?" Without answering, he handed me a biscuit that I quickly gobbled. The cop then asked me a bunch of questions that I didn't answer. I remember seeing a few movies where the gangsters never told the cops anything, so I figured this was the right thing to do. Deep down I realized I'd be going back to school and would probably get a good punishment for running away. After a while, another cop came in and told the other policeman I was another one of those runaways from St. Mary's. Shortly thereafter a fat brother, I think his name was Richard, arrived at the police station and without too much conversation jerked me into a waiting car.

For running away, I got the worst whipping of my life. A thick wooden switch was used, and it left scars and welts on my legs and rear end. It hurt for days afterward. Elwood and Willy said it just wasn't right for them to give me such a beating. However, the worst punishment was not the beating but standing on a rock. For running away, I had to stand on a small rock every day for two weeks at recess time. While everyone else was playing, I had to stand on a stone. The rock was located outside an office where the brothers hung out at recess, so they watched me. The standing stone was round and about the size of a football, so it was difficult to stay balanced, especially with guys pretending to push me off. If there was rain or snow, I still had to stand on the rock, and it easily got slippery. Even though our recess was only about thirty or forty minutes, it was extremely tough to stay balanced. If any of the brothers saw me get off the rock, an extra day was added to my punishment. I don't remember exactly, but the first week I got off the rock a number of times and got extra days punishment whenever a brother saw me. Balancing and remaining motionless hurt my legs as I stood on that damn rock. If I dared swat a bug in my face, I lost my balance. The second week I learned how to ignore the fellas teasing me and the strain of standing like a statue. What I eventually did was daydream about ice cream, toys, big delicious meals, home, and other nice stuff. I would even close my eyes and almost not hear the boys screaming. Well, after almost four weeks, the brothers let me off the rock punishment. They asked me if I had learned my lesson, and I lied and told them what they wanted to hear.

Shortly after the rock torture, a very good thing happened. Elwood began to play the clarinet in the school band, and he told me I should join. He played pretty well, but I never tried or cared much about music. But when he explained the band would soon take trips to play at college football games, I liked the idea very much. I especially relished the thought of getting away from St. Mary's. I went to a practice, and the brother in charge asked if I would like to play a piccolo. He gave me a piccolo and told me to practice. Elwood tried to help, but frankly I was never very good. During practice, the brother in charge would look my way when I was tooting and frown. I learned a little about the notes and ways to play but never improved much. Elwood told me to not play too loud, so I barely blew into the piccolo. Luckily I got to travel with the band, and it was terrific. We got to watch college football games, march and play at halftime, and mess around on the bus. I remember we played at Notre Dame, Army, and Navy games. They had huge crowds, and it was exciting to watch the game and see all the fans whooping and hollering. We also got plenty to eat when we traveled. There were always hot dogs, soda pop, burgers, peanuts, and popcorn for everybody. I thought the chow was better than the crap we were fed at school.

I recall one day getting ready to board the bus for a game in Philadelphia when a bunch of photographers gathered up the band. Then a big fancy sedan pulled up. To our surprise Babe Ruth stepped out of the car and waved. Everybody cheered the Bambino. I had heard that years earlier, before he became a big baseball star, he attended St. Mary's. We were told the Babe gave our school a lot of money and paid for our band instruments and outfits. After the photos, Babe Ruth went around and shook our hands and gave us each a signed baseball card. It was a pretty exciting day. Somebody told me later that Babe Ruth was an orphan and a tough kid when he attended St. Mary's. This got me to thinking that this rough place might not be such a bad place after all. I felt proud that I was in the same school as this famous sports hero. Our band also played and attended a few baseball games in Baltimore and other towns where Babe Ruth played.

Despite skimpy meals, occasional fistfights, and our mean teachers, things seemed to get better. The band trips, the extra food Willy pilfered, and my increasing ability to hold my own in fights were all good things that helped me slowly feel better about the place. One day Elwood told me I was getting a good reputation because I was considered fearless and not afraid of bigger boys. Since I continued to be smaller than others, this made me proud. I was about twelve or thirteen at this time and stopped feeling so blue about being away from home. Willy was giving me some of his smokes, and since my behavior had improved, I was getting chances to leave school and visit the city. I guess it was about this time I started noticing and flirting with girls I saw around town, but most of the time they ignored me or giggled like hyenas when I winked or smiled at them.

Since things were going nicely, things had to change and they did. One day the principal called us in and told us our time at St. Mary's was over, and we'd be going home. Although our grandparents and Uncle Joe had visited us at Christmas a few times, we hadn't lived at home in about eight or nine years. Sure enough, within a week or so, one of the brothers had us gather up our stuff in paper sacks. He took us to the train station, pinned tags on our shirts, and told us to behave and not get off the train until we reached Portsmouth. Granddaddy Arthur Culpepper met us at the station and took us to his home on Race Avenue in the Westhaven section of town. He told us we would be living there with his family, which consisted of my grandparents, Uncle Joe, and Aunts Essie and Mary. Elwood asked if there would be room for the three of us in his little house. Grandpa told us there wasn't enough room so he had fixed up the garage and it would be our new home.

The Culpepper's were my mother's family. We were told our father was unable to raise us due to his whipping and head injuries. Grandma told me my daddy couldn't raise five kids since he could hardly take care of himself. Our father's name was Lemuel, but most folks called him Lamb because he was a gentle and peaceful person. He had twinkling blue eyes and an angelic smile. He liked to dress up in a suit, vest, and tie every Sunday for dinner. He liked to tell Bible stories and smiled when we related our adventures at St. Vincent's and St. Mary's. He was a very religious person but never attended the same church every week. People joked that he might visit St. Paul's one Sunday and then attend a Pentecostal service the next Sunday with some of his colored friends. Occasionally, on a Saturday, he would even attend a local synagogue. He didn't drive, but he walked a lot and got free rides from bus drivers around town who knew him. Sometimes he forgot our names or got them mixed up, but we all knew it was because of his severe beating, and we just laughed and accepted whatever name he called us.

In our new garage home, Granddaddy had covered the oily dirt floor with some old carpet and cardboard. He installed a small, wood-burning iron stove and used some sheets to cover the windows. Cracks in the old garage door were stuffed with wads of newspaper, and a single light bulb dangled from the ceiling. The space had a bed made up of two mattresses, two chairs, a small wooden table with a wash bowl, and several boxes for our clothes and stuff. He moved his tools and other things to the rear of the garage to give us more room and forbade us from messing with his tools. Grandpa told us our meals and baths would be taken in the house, and the garage would be our sleeping and homework quarters. The garage was drafty and smelly, but it was our new home, and best of all, we didn't have to share it with a bunch of other boys.

I slept between Willy and Elwood, which was good especially on the cold nights. When the weather was warm, we opened the windows and door to catch any breezes. The roof had a few leaks but no drips over our bed. Since we were near a swampy creek, we got plenty of gnats, mosquitoes, and other bugs buzzing around. Occasionally we would see and chase mice running around, but they were small. Some weekends Granddaddy took us fishing in a neighbor's rowboat on the Elizabeth River near City Park. I remember one time, when I got the chance to row, I dropped an oar. While my grandfather cussed me a blue streak, Willy jumped in the water and retrieved the oar. Everybody had a good laugh, and I got plenty of ribbing as the story was retold to my grandma and others. We used handlines and a dip net and usually caught enough fish or crabs for a meal. Granddaddy and Elwood were the best fishermen, always catching the biggest and most fish or crabs. Granny would fry up the fish in lard or boil the crabs, and this always gave us a tasty seafood dinner. We ate our meals, listened to the radio, and used the bathroom in the house while sleeping and doing our homework in the garage. It all worked out okay and was sure better than dealing with a bunch of other boys at the orphanage schools.

My brothers and I were baptized Catholic, and my grandparents, who were also Catholic, were strict about us attending church. Every Sunday and on all the holy days of obligation, we would squeeze into Granddaddy's old sedan and go downtown to St. Paul's Church. They also enrolled us at

St. Joseph's Academy. Since they didn't have money for our daily bus fare, we thumbed, walked, and biked our way to school, which was a few miles away. St. Joseph's had teaching nuns, and they were much nicer than the brothers at St. Mary's. Overall, I guess you could say I was an average student. Elwood was smarter and got As, while Willy liked to skip classes and got called on the carpet many times. My favorite classes were math and history, but the thing I liked most was the presence of girls.

I was in my early teens about this time and began running around with guys in the Westhaven neighborhood. Elwood and Willy had begun dating girls and had buddies with jalopies, so I was on my own around the neighborhood. The fellows I ran into were tough characters, and our arguments usually turned into fights. Since I was somewhat experienced in the fighting department, I quickly earned a reputation as a good scrapper. We called ourselves commandos but were actually what you might call juvenile delinquents. With a few pals, I got together a little gang, and we walked around looking for or making trouble with other boys. Brawling with guys from other neighborhoods and picking fights just for the hell of it got us street respect and more than a few tongue lashings from older folks and cops. None of us had guns or knives and relied on our wrestling and fighting skills to overpower our opponents. A couple of times, crawling through store windows at night, we stole candy, bottles of beer, and smokes. Once we broke into a school and swiped a little box of lunch money that we split up and used to buy soda, comic books, and cigarettes. Also, about this time I began to share some of my loot with a few girls. I "scatted" around with a few young ladies and did my share of smooching, petting, and other crazy stuff. My commandos and I broke out streetlights, tipped trash cans, knocked mailboxes down, and did other dumb things. We began to get a lot of attention from coppers tooling around in their patrol cars. They began watching us closely and questioning us whenever anything bad happened in the neighborhood.

One afternoon, my boys and I were in a watermelon patch eating and smashing melons. The field was near a railroad track, and when we saw a passenger train approaching, one of the guys dared me to throw a melon at the train. Never one to chicken out on a dare, I threw a big chunk of melon, and to my surprise it hit and shattered a passenger car window. People at the window screamed, and, needless to say, we all ran like hell. A few days later, a police detective came by our house and was waiting for me when I returned from school. The cop told my grandparents about the incident, which included several passengers getting cuts from the broken glass, and their suspicion of my involvement. To all his questions I lied, and my buddies all lied too when they were questioned. Nobody in our gang ratted me out, and I felt pretty lucky. Even though my boys and I continued to raise hell and fight, I felt bad about what I had done and gradually eased away from this period of rowdiness.

When I was finishing my tenth year of high school, Grandma announced that I'd had enough education, and it was now time for me to get a job and help the family. She pulled me out of St. Joseph's and told me her son Joe had two years of high school, and two years was enough for him and enough for me too. Joe had gotten a decent job driving a beer truck. Back then, during the Depression, everyone in the house had jobs and was expected to give Grandma some money for groceries and household bills. Everybody was expected to help, and that's why she pulled my brothers out of school before they could graduate too. Elwood had gotten a job as a painter's helper, and Willy was doing odd jobs around town. I didn't want to leave school, but she didn't give any of us a choice. When Grandma made up her mind, it was pointless to disagree. So my formal education ended when I was about to go into the eleventh grade. I got my first job downtown as a Western Union messenger boy. They supplied me with a bicycle to carry telegrams to homes and businesses all over town. Every day I cycled many miles doing this job, and the pay was a few dollars a week and any tips, which were rare. Grandma didn't ask about my tips, which usually only amounted to a little change, but she did take my pay envelope and only gave me a dollar and any coins. She insisted that we were lucky to have a roof over our heads, and everyone had to do their part to pay the bills.

I didn't understand a lot about the Depression but knew times were tough for a lot of folks. I remember seeing families living in tents and little shacks all around town, and every day I would see men sleeping in alleys and on park benches. While some may have been hobos or drunks, many were simply regular fellows flat broke and without a job. I also remember at this time seeing lines of people outside of churches and other places waiting for food or clothing handouts. Granddaddy Arthur had steady work as a shipyard carpenter while everyone else in the family had little jobs to make money. Grandma Lula didn't have a job but managed the bills, groceries, and laundry, and took care of things around the house. Despite living in a drafty garage, always wearing hand-me-downs, and never having much money, I considered my brothers and me to be pretty lucky compared to others.

A few weeks after my seventeenth birthday, Grandma and Grandpa called me into the kitchen for a serious talk. Without any conversation, I was told that I'd been signed up for the Civilian Conservation Corps and would be leaving for the mountains in a week. I didn't know anything about the CCC except that Elwood had been sent out West about a year earlier and, according to my grandparents, was doing just fine. Grandma said since I had just turned seventeen, I was now old enough, and it was an excellent way to make more money than working as a telegram boy. The pay was twenty-five dollars a month, and my grandparents set it up so twenty dollars would be sent to them each month, and I could keep five bucks. They told me the CCC outfit would provide clothes, shelter, and meals, so they felt five dollars a month was more than enough spending money for me. Like so many things in my life up to this point, I didn't get much of a say in the decision but trusted my grandparents. I always felt they would do the right thing for me and my brothers. The day before I left, my father and several of his sisters joined us at the Culpepper's for a nice going-away Sunday dinner. I never saw much of my daddy's people, and they seemed like nice folks, but I sensed the Culpepper's and Father's people didn't get along too well.

After a sweltering, bumpy train ride, I ended up in Wytheville along with other fellows heading to the CCC camp. A bus took us off the paved highway, up winding dusty roads, and then to a clear spot up in the hills. Right away we were assigned bunks in a one-story wooden building and were issued shirts, pants, boots, underwear, and socks. In the chow hall at an assembly, a tall, older man welcomed everyone and told us the CCC camp was a government plan to get young men paying jobs by doing useful things. We were warned that fighting, liquor, and women were not allowed at the camp and could get us fined, expelled, and a trip to the local jail. For the first time, I learned that CCC meant Civilian Conservation Corps. Our work involved clearing forests for new roads, logging, repairing old roads, clearing brush and rocks, and assisting firefighters whenever possible. The work was tough. In the summer it was sweltering, but by November the snow and cold left me chilled. Working on loose rocks, around fallen trees, and near fires was treacherous and sometimes dangerous. A misstep along the ridges gave everybody cuts and bruises, and once in a while, unlucky guys ended up with broken arms or legs from their falls.

Out in the hills I saw a lot of wildlife. Whitetail deer, hawks, coons, rabbits, snakes, foxes, and other small critters appeared almost every day. We knew there were also bears nearby. Their scat and deep paw prints were everywhere; however, actual sightings were rare. It was at this time that I became very interested in snakes, and there were certainly plenty of them around. I liked watching the thin, long green ones and the fat rattlers and copperheads slither their way through the grass or sneak into or over bushes. They were fast and silent, except when surprised or disturbed. When startled, the dangerous snakes gathered themselves in coils and would either feign or hurl themselves into an attack. Everyone was warned and instructed on identifying the poisonous ones and told how to kill them, which would prevent a buddy from getting bit. I was fascinated by the snakes, and once in a while I'd catch a harmless one, stuff it in my pocket, and use it to scare some of the boys.

At our camp we got three squares a day, and the food was plentiful and good. I always had a great appetite after a long day of hiking and forestry chores. The tents and cabins were good, except during the heavy rainstorms or on the coldest days when we had to avoid roof leaks and freezing drafts. After working from sunrise to sunset almost six days a week, most everybody simply wanted to wash up, eat, have a smoke, and sleep. However, there was a little building with card tables, games, and a few magazines, which they called our rec room. This is where trouble sometimes started because guys let their arguments over cards, their manliness, or their girlfriends turn into fistfights. Things here were similar to the neighborhood and orphanage brawls I had witnessed since my boyhood. I got into a few fights and gave as good as I got. In other words, I wasn't a pushover and made sure the other fellow got a busted lip, a shiner, or a bloody nose in return for the beating I received. At the CCC camp, I began to believe that I was living in a dog-eat-dog world, which meant the tough guys survived while the weak fellows were doomed.

We worked five and a half days, unless there was a fire, and everyone talked and looked forward to the weekend. The nearest town was Bluefield. On Saturday afternoon, after washing up and donning our best shirt and pants, one of the bosses would drive the bus to town. I usually had about a dollar and a few coins in spending money, unless I had been lucky or unlucky playing craps or cards. When I was flat broke, there were a couple of buddies willing to lend me enough change for the visit to town. First thing, I'd buy a pint of white lightning and smokes. Booze was about twenty-five cents a pint and cigarettes ten or fifteen cents a pack. After getting half-looped, there were always whores hanging around the bars to fuss or fight over. The girls were local women out to have a laugh and get free drinks. One crazy night, I gave up my virginity to an old hag about forty years old. It wasn't unusual for some of the fights to get out of hand, which resulted in a few boys ending up in jail for the night. I'm sure some of the young men from the CCC visited the local library or enjoyed a nice dinner at a restaurant, but frankly I didn't know too many of those guys. While one could catch the late bus back to camp, most spent the night in town and returned Sunday. In addition to the local churches, the camp had a Sunday service. Sad to say, I usually spent Sunday sobering up and sleeping. I spent two years in the CCC, and it was a good experience. I feel like I went in as a boy and came out as a man, even though I was still a teenager.

At Saint Vincent's Orphanage

Charles (Dinky) - teenager

Catherine (Kakie) - teenager

Love - Waiting for War

When I got back to Westhaven, a few surprises awaited. Willy and Elwood had moved out of the garage. For a short while, I lived alone in the garage apartment, but my grandparents told me it was time I moved out and got out on my own. They didn't kick me out but reminded me daily. Since Elwood and Willy had moved away, things just weren't the same at the Culpepper's. Willy was doing all kinds of odd jobs around town. I remember one day walking down High Street and hearing, "Dinky, hey Dinky." I looked up and down the street but saw no one. However, I kept hearing my name shouted. Finally, I heard, "Up here, up here." I looked up, and near the top of the St. Paul's steeple I saw Willy. He was as green as the steeple he was slathering with green paint. Dangling from a rope ladder, he waved and smiled. I yelled to him that he was a jackass because what he was doing looked mighty dangerous. But he just laughed and resumed sloshing paint all over the steeple and himself. Whether he was doing yard work, repairing a fence, or painting, Willy always had a quick smile. Back then, he seemed to be easier going and more mischievous than Elwood or me. At this time Willy was living with friends downtown.

Elwood was a big surprise when he married his girlfriend, Martha Bernard, and moved into a little apartment on Clifford Street. Martha was a very friendly and pretty girl and different from Elwood, who was quiet and serious. Despite their differences, they seemed to be a happy couple. About this same time, Elwood had gotten a position at the naval shipyard as a helper in the paint shop. He told me about the steady pay and benefits of his new job and insisted I should apply. I resisted, but since I needed a few fast bucks in my pocket, I accepted an offer from my Uncle Joe. He drove a beer truck and took me on as his helper. For my part of the job, I ended up hauling the heavy kegs into every beer joint and honky-tonk in town while Joe flirted with every woman in sight and acted like a big shot. But it was all right because I was strong, and it was nice to make money without Grandma taking a huge cut of my pay. Eventually Elwood and Martha invited me to move in with them for free until I got my feet on the ground and my own place. It was a generous offer, and I readily accepted. Elwood again encouraged me to apply for a job at the shipyard, which was a short walk from where they lived. He got me the application papers, I applied, and a few weeks later, I got a letter approving me for a general laborer job. My pay was twelve dollars a week, which at the time seemed like a fortune. Back then, a pack of Lucky Strikes cost a nickel, bread was seven cents a loaf, a pint of whiskey cost a quarter, bologna ran ten cents a pound, and a movie ticket was about a dime. For the first time in my life, I had enough cash to buy the things I wanted with enough left over to help my brother and sister-in-law with their groceries and other expenses.

Finally moving out of the garage, I had my own bedroom at my brother's place and started a new, decent-paying job. I began to feel things were going well, and I liked the independence and not being under my grandparents' control. While I was thankful my grandparents had taken care of me, I was now a man and felt it was time to make my own way. It was terrific to occasionally buy a new shirt, some groceries, and have a few extra bucks in my pocket for smokes or a beer. At this time, I was seeing a few different girls but nothing serious. I had stopped going to church, but I maintained the strong beliefs I learned as a kid. Even though I wasn't a gangster, I still hung with some of the rough boys from Westhaven, gambled a little, occasionally gave or got an ass-whipping, and mostly dated what might be called "easy women." Little did I realize that only a few blocks away lived a girlfriend of Martha's who would become the most important part of my life. She would mark a big turning point for the rest of my days. This was about 1940, and I was twenty-one years old.

After a few months, Elwood and I got postcards ordering us to report to the main post office to register for the draft. When we got our physicals, they found Elwood had a foot problem. The lucky sucker was disqualified from the draft and any military service. I was classified as 1A, which meant I was healthy and 100 percent qualified for the draft. Meanwhile, Willy had enlisted in the army a year or two earlier on his own. The talk of war was all over the front pages and on the radio. I didn't pay much attention and never connected the increased work and overtime hours at the shipyard with the chance that we'd get mixed up in a war. Frankly, I thought it was all too far away and the troubles the Germans and

Japanese were causing would never affect me or the United States. I had never thought much about war and enjoyed cowboy movies more than war movies. However, I remember seeing an old movie entitled *All's Quiet on the Western Front*, about a bunch of pals who joined the army during World War I. They were cheered and paraded as heroes by their hometown folks, but once they got into combat, they were all killed. It was a sad and gruesome story and left me hoping to never get involved in any kind of war.

One night, Martha introduced me to one of her girlfriends at a neighborhood picnic. Her name was Catherine Lee Williams, but I have to admit my first impressions of her were not so good. At first I thought she was a little dull because she was different from most of the women I had been around. She didn't smoke, drink, or cuss, and I quickly discovered she wasn't "fast" or appreciative of my moves. But I sensed she liked me, and to my surprise I was intrigued because she was sweet, nice, and so different from most of the girls and women I had known. Despite my rude and clumsy beginning, we gradually got to be friends. After a few weeks, Martha told me she thought Catherine had taken a shine to me. Catherine's family lived close to Elwood and Martha, so it was easy to drop by her house to visit or just sit and chat on her front porch. We talked about anything and everything under the sun. She told me about her love of cats, and I told her about the orphanages and the nuns and brothers who had been my teachers. We got to know each other a little more with each encounter.

As we got together more, I realized she was the nicest girl I had ever met, but I probably wasn't good enough for her.

Nonetheless, the attraction was mutual, and soon, almost every afternoon or early evening after my work day, we got together for a chat and hand-holding. I wanted to kiss her but was afraid she would think I was being too forward. Finally, one afternoon she invited me to Sunday dinner to meet her parents and family. I had briefly met her mother, brother, sisters, and a few other relatives as they passed us on the front porch of Catherine's home. She had a big family, and unlike mine they all were constantly in touch with each other. Her home was average sized, and her folks were regular working people. Everyone I met from her family was polite, and it was all pretty casual. However, I had yet to meet or encounter her father, and I had no idea if I could sit down with so many people, handle myself in a decent way, and not come across as a jackass. As the big Sunday dinner date approached, I began to sweat things out, wondering if I would be accepted. I almost made an excuse to skip dinner since they seemed so much nicer than my roughneck friends. I honestly wasn't sure I had the manners and confidence to blend in with these nice, normal folks. One day I confessed to Catherine all my misdeeds as a teenager and my run-ins with cops because I didn't want her to find out later and drop me like a hot potato. She laughed and told me that Martha had already told her all those stories, and none of it was a big deal to her. I think Catherine sensed my doubts and told me not to worry because no matter what might happen, she would still be fond of me. I began to have strong feelings for her and determined that an encounter with and questions from her family would only strengthen our friendship. During those last few days before that Sunday, I just couldn't stop thinking about Catherine's quiet charm, soft voice, and gentle touch. For the first time in my life, I felt we might be a good couple and that she was the best person for me to marry. I believe about this time I fell in love with her. Strangely, I couldn't get her off my mind at work and got clumsy, stumbled over things, dropped my tools left and right, and wasn't very hungry at lunchtime. My boss thought I was sick, but I knew the real reason for my distraction was my constant daydreaming about Catherine.

Elwood lent me a very nice flowered tie, one of his suits, and a fine pair of shiny shoes for my big day. Martha pinned up the pants since I was two or three inches shorter than Elwood. Ready to go, I inspected myself in a mirror and thought the suit was a little droopy, but not too bad. From somewhere Martha produced a red rosebud and pinned it to my coat lapel. Elwood shook my hand and wished me good luck, and Martha gave me a big hug. I left their apartment with a good sense of confidence about Sunday dinner with the Williams's family. Catherine met me at the front door, and for the first time, she gave me a quick little kiss on the cheek. My heart soared, and I felt like a million bucks. She ushered me into the living room where everyone was sitting. They had just returned from church, and I was introduced to her family. I shook her brother's hand, made a slight bow to her sisters as they choked back giggles, and shook hands with her brothers-in-law. Her mother, Lucy, gave me a beautiful smile upon our official introduction, and her father nodded with a small frown and quickly shot me a question: "So you're a Catholic?" Before I could answer, Mrs. Williams scolded him and announced it was time to eat. Catherine grabbed my hand and squeezed it hard as we all sat down. The aroma of fried chicken mixed with fresh cooked vegetables and bread was the best food smell I had experienced in a long time. After a rambling grace by Mr. Williams, we ate and, boy, oh boy, was it a feast. Thankfully there wasn't much talk at the table, and I momentarily forgot the threatening tone of Mr. Williams's question and enjoyed the sumptuous meal.

After seconds and an outstanding chunk of freshly baked apple pie, the meal ended. We quit the dining room, and while some drifted out to the front porch, Catherine guided me to the living room where her parents sat. Catherine and her mother did most of the talking. They allowed me to reveal my past situations, current situation, and plans for the future. Mrs. Williams's questions and comments were gentle, and though she was a hardworking woman, she carried a grace and beauty I could see clearly in her daughter. After a period of casual conversation, Mr. Williams decided to speak. He again questioned my religion, and I answered best I could. He stated, despite interruptions from his wife, that he didn't care for papists and wasn't sure I'd be welcome in his home in the future. As Catherine and her mother gasped and I turned purple, Mr. John Williams pulled himself out of his rocker and left the room. When he left, Mrs. Williams whispered not to worry because she thought John would come around in time. I later learned that the Williams family were Baptists of the strictest variety. They supposedly didn't like jazzy music, dancing, liquor drinking, or smoking. Well, I liked all those things, and I eventually found out that many in the Williams clan liked those things too. I lingered with Catherine on the front porch till the evening, and despite the stares and smirks from her younger sisters, we enjoyed what you might call our first official date.

Many a time after work I'd meet Catherine at Wood's Bakery where she worked. They had delicious cinnamon buns and pastries, but of course she was the real reason for my visits. We also spent many hours on the steps or porch of her Lansing Avenue home. After a time, Mr. Williams began to nod when we passed and finally told me I was welcome to eat there when I wanted because there was usually enough food. After a lot of worry, I began to feel Mr. Williams had accepted me despite our religious differences. Catherine's mother always insisted I eat a second portion at meals and often fussed that I was a "skinny old thing." I gladly ate whatever she served. I got to know Catherine's daddy too. He was a short, stout, and muscular man. He was a butcher for a meat company owned by one of his brothers. He was generally quiet, but when he spoke, everyone around the table or house hushed up and listened. I remember one Sunday after dinner he took me out to his shed, pulled out a wooden box from under a workbench, and offered me one of his cigars and a swig from a pint of whiskey. At first I was stunned and thought the old man was testing me, but he chuckled and assured me he was on the level. From that time on, we got along fine and occasionally enjoyed his hidden, sinful vices in the shed.

Catherine and I got to be what they used to call a regular item in her neighborhood because we were always together. Playing children would tease us as we walked down the street, and people our age would sometimes hoot at us and grin. Some of Catherine's sisters were already married, and we earnestly began to talk about marriage. I loved her dearly, but since I was still living with my brother and didn't have much money, I was a little scared about the responsibilities of marriage. I wanted us to have our own little place with decent furniture, surrounded by a nice white fence, but on a laborer's wage, I didn't know if I could give her all the nice things she deserved. By now I had gotten to know her family and felt comfortable with them all. I was especially fond of her mother, Lucy, who was a genuinely warm person in addition to being a terrific cook. I never had a mother and thought she was the ideal mother I wish I could have enjoyed. Catherine was a great lover of critters. She had names for the neighborhood raccoons and squirrels and was never afraid of strange, barking dogs or menacing cats. She held a special affection for cats. Around her house there were always a few stray pusses and their kittens, and Catherine adored and pampered them all. She would deliver table scraps and bowls of water once or twice a day to her cats. Family members and neighbors nicknamed her "Kitty," and the little kids in the family who struggled to say Kitty turned it into "Kakie." Most knew my nickname, so sometimes when seen together we were greeted by the old rhyme "Kitty and Dinky sitting in a tree ... blah, blah, blah." The teasing didn't bother us one iota. Eventually I joined Catherine in her love for cats, even though as a young ruffian I had been a tormentor and scourge to felines. Our talk of marriage became part of our daily conversations. I was putting a little money aside every week and constantly checking the shipyard employment office for better-paying trade jobs or apprenticeships.

This was early 1941, and Hitler was raising hell in Europe. According to Elwood, despite Roosevelt's promises, he thought we might end up getting into the war. Also, in the news I saw where the Japanese were at war with China, and the situation in Asia looked pretty bad. I was eligible for the draft and began to wonder if I'd be called to serve. About this time Catherine was asked to go down to Florida and help an aunt who was recuperating from a serious operation. She was only gone a few weeks, but during her absence I realized how much I missed her company. We exchanged a few postcards, and I got lonely and down in the dumps missing her touch, our smooching, her pretty blue eyes, and her lovely face. During our time apart, I told myself, whether rich or poor, we would get married when she got home. Even though I didn't have much money, I made a down payment and got a loan on an engagement and wedding ring.

When Kakie got home, I proposed, and she tearfully and joyfully agreed. Her acceptance made me happy as a lark and proud that we would soon be a married couple. I approached her father and asked his permission. Even though this was an old-fashioned practice, I thought it was an important thing to do. To my relief he gave his consent, crushed my hand in a handshake, and welcomed me into his family. I told Catherine that while she was in Florida my draft notice had arrived, and I wasn't sure about my reporting date. I discussed with her my concern that we should perhaps wait on marriage until I got my military service out of the way. I knew going in the army might keep me away from Portsmouth and felt this would be a terrible burden on her, but Catherine insisted we get married before I was ordered to boot camp. While I wasn't keen on getting married right away, she fretted, so we set our wedding date.

On May 15, 1941, at a little Baptist church in Cradock, we celebrated our marriage vows with family and friends in attendance. We had no honeymoon and immediately moved in with Elwood and Martha. Even though we didn't have our own place, this was a very happy time. I felt like the luckiest man in the world and avoided thinking about leaving my beautiful young bride. Then the army sent a telegram with orders to report for basic training on May 27. Our new married life was coming to a temporary end after less than two weeks, but we laughed and loved our way every hour of every day before my departure. Finally, the day arrived, and I packed a little bag and said goodbye to my new in-laws, brothers, and friends. Mrs. Williams and her sisters were tearful, and the family men offered handshakes and encouragement, saying my absence would be short-lived. They all assured me if war came, it wouldn't last long, and I'd be home soon enough. I wasn't sure about how a war might go but was damn sure I wanted to quickly finish my military service and rush back to my wonderful new wife and her fine family. Having spent much of my life bouncing around between orphanages, the CCC camp, and living in a garage, I felt the army was just another bump in the road I would have to endure before settling down to a normal life with Catherine.

Elwood drove me to the bus station with Catherine and Martha. We did our best to laugh and joke, but when the Greyhound honked signaling everyone to board, Kakie got very quiet and then cried like a baby. Our last embraces and kisses were sweet but difficult. She was bawling, and I was fighting the urge to shed a few of my own tears. I kept promising her I wouldn't be gone long and everything would be all right. I assured her we'd soon get our own little place, maybe have a few kids, and definitely have a houseful of cats and dogs. Her beautiful, moist blue eyes locked into mine, and as she nodded, I felt a sudden rush of immense joy and sadness. On board, I lowered the grimy window and gave a little wave. I fought the urge to jump off the bus and rush back into her waiting arms, but I couldn't and didn't. With a groan and a puff of gray diesel smoke, the bus jerked away.

Catherine and Charles

Catherine and Charles - wedding day

Charles and fellow recruit at Ft. Belvoir Va.

Tom Pasquel

Army and the Philippines

The bus was loaded with others heading for military service. I noticed a few local boys I had known around Portsmouth and Norfolk County. Several old pals I ran with from Westhaven and St. Joseph's Academy were also on board. We stopped in Suffolk and picked up a few more men before heading to Richmond. In a huge building, army men shuffled us through endless lines. We were told to undress and stood around stark naked waiting for physical exams, and shortly thereafter we got needles pricking our rear ends. Next, they had us fill out and sign a bunch of forms and answer a lot of crazy questions. We were then ordered to complete little test booklets with puzzles, math, and English questions. In a large hall, a decorated army officer had us stand at attention and repeat the oath of enlistment. The captain congratulated us, and everyone cheered. Finally, we were hustled into another line where we got our orders and a box lunch as we clambered aboard a green army bus.

Our next stop was announced by a skinny sergeant who joined our group in Richmond. We were heading to Fort

Meade, Maryland, for testing and classification. After a while, the bus got quiet as we bumped along US 1 heading north. Out the window, as the sun began its descent, I got homesick for Kakie and home. This was a new experience for me. I had never felt such loneliness when I was away at the orphanages and CCC camp.

We spent several days at Fort Meade. They put us in barracks and had us "falling in and falling out" every few hours as we were marched off for testing and classification. I had one examiner ask me if I liked other guys and if I was a Nazi or Communist. A lieutenant asked me what I saw in a bunch of weird ink blotches. Eventually I tired of the questions and wondered if there were any correct answers. On a few occasions, I felt like smacking some of the questioners in the snoot because I thought their questions were insulting or downright stupid. But I did the right thing and kept my mouth shut. My early military impressions reminded me of things I had experienced at the orphanages and CCC camp. A bunch of guys and long lines waiting to get chow, take a crap, shave, or shower. There was no fighting but probably because there were so many noncoms watching and waiting for anyone to get frisky.

On the third day at Fort Meade, we finished testing and got our orders. I was being sent to Fort Belvoir, Virginia, for basic training. I sent a penny postcard to Kakie to let her know where I would be for the next few months. Some of the guys I knew were heading for camps in Louisiana, Texas, New Jersey, and other distant places. I felt lucky to remain in state and not too far from home. They loaded us aboard another army bus for the short trip to Belvoir. After reaching the post, we were herded into more lines. First, we got scalped by barbers, and everyone laughed at each other's new baldness. Next, they issued us gear, which ranged from underwear to boots and canteens. Lugging our full duffel bags, we got assigned to one of several old, white-washed barracks buildings. After a few days, my civvies were getting stinky, so I was happy to change into some of my new GI duds. On the first day, a burly platoon sergeant came in and ordered us to shave, shit, shower, and prepare to assemble for mess call. He jokingly mentioned that he wanted everyone to enjoy this "vacation" day because it would be our last one for a while. Later I hit the sack and dreamed about Catherine and hoped she might be thinking of me too. Next morning came quick as the bugling and shouting got everyone up as the sun was barely rising. Like a bunch of chickens with their heads chopped off, we flopped around getting dressed and making our beds. After the first few days, we got into a pattern, and things were less frantic.

I honestly don't remember a lot about boot camp except that it was a daily routine of calisthenics, classes, inspections, chow, drills with bayoneted rifles, hand-to-hand combat, obstacle courses, and then more calisthenics. I qualified with the M1 rifle but also fired old Enfields and Springfield relics from World War I or maybe the Spanish American War. The training became a blur of activity except when it rained. I think our instructors were thrilled when we had to march or crawl through mud puddles. A few evenings a week we got to watch a movie after mess hall, and the newsreels became our main source of information.

By the middle of 1941, things were looking pretty bad. England and a lot of European countries were getting a terrible beating from Hitler. The Chinese and some of their neighbors were suffering at the hands of the Japanese. Although I took some comfort in the wide oceans that separated us from Germany and Japan, I began to worry that those suckers might just draw us into war. A bunch of rumors were floating around about peace treaties and secret invasions, but except for the newsreels, I thought most of what I heard was baloney. After a few weeks of basic, several men were whispering about bugging out. They hated the army and wanted to go home. One or two guys from our platoon actually took off but within a few days were caught. They got written up and assigned nasty duties, such as latrine cleaning and garbage collecting. Except for being separated from Catherine, I felt I was doing my duty, and I think the majority of others felt the same way.

During boot camp, I did my best to send out a letter or postcard every few days to Kakie. Our trainers kept us hustling night and day, and sometimes I was too tired to do anything but flop into my bunk. I received a note or letter from her every few days, and inhaling the scent of her perfume or lipstick on the letter or envelope was always the highlight of my day. I did all right with the basic training, which ended with a long march carrying a rifle, full knapsack, and load of gear. We were promised a weekend pass if we survived this test, and I was tickled pink with the chance to get home and see my bride. I was excited on the way home and felt I looked pretty sharp in my new olive-drab dress uniform. The reunion with Kakie was wonderful. Her mother said she was worried that I was getting too skinny and urged me to have large portions and seconds. I felt good and proud about my accomplishments and new status as a soldier. Naturally I spent most of my time with Catherine. Our time together was the best part of my leave. We talked more about someday getting our own little love nest and the vegetables and flowers we might plant. We thumbed through magazines, choosing the furniture and furnishings for our dream home. We talked about the children, cats, and dogs that would someday fill our home. Neither of us did much sleeping and sat up late into the night talking and planning the years ahead.

Enjoying such a great visit, I stupidly overslept and missed my scheduled bus back to Belvoir. I caught a later Trailways, and though I ran like hell from the terminal, I was several hours late getting back to my barracks. My platoon sergeant was waiting and gave me holy hell and commanded me to stand at attention during his long lecture. He roared about the rules and the fact I was AWOL (absent without leave) and could be sent to the stockade or kicked out of the army. I felt pretty bad, and when he stopped shouting, he allowed me a chance to speak. His scowl remained fixed as I meekly spit out my excuses. Silence followed for a few minutes, and to my relief, the old man allowed a slight grin and grunt and then told me to get the hell out of his sight and never go AWOL again. I forget his name, but he was a grizzled World War I veteran, and while he regularly scared the hell out of us, he did a good job with our training.

After a few more months of training, I got assigned as a replacement troop for the 803rd Aviation Engineer Battalion. I was assigned a light truck driver job, and my assignment was to help others in keeping army/air corps fields clear. Back in those days, before the Air Force became a separate branch, the army and navy flew and maintained all the military planes. Parts often fell off the older models when they took off or landed, and our mission was to ensure the runways were always clear. Junk on the airstrip could easily wreck an airplane or cause tires to blow out. On the paved runways, we also cleaned up oil and fluid spills, patched ruts, filled holes, smoothed out bumps, cleared weeds, and generally kept the runways usable. The smaller single-engine planes were nimble, and it didn't take much to tip one over if it ran into any crap on the runway. If a pilot complained about anything, we were ordered to quickly fix the problem. Several times we were also issued shotguns and ordered to scare off flocks of seagulls, which occasionally flew into propellers. We also kept the hangars clean. The work wasn't hard, and I got along with most of the fellows in my company. Once in a while, some hotshot pilot would piss and moan so much that our platoon sergeant would get on our backs and demand we work harder or faster.

I'd say the majority of us came in under the draft, and only a handful were veterans or volunteers. I was assigned to Company B, and it was an interesting mix of men from all over the country. It took a while to understand some of their accents and mannerisms, and I'm certain they may have found my manner of speaking strange. Despite our differences, we all got along. I bunked above a boy who became my army buddy for the next few years. His name was Thomas Pasquel, and I called him Tom or Tommy. He was from the upstate New York town of Tuckahoe. He was a bachelor with plans to marry his girlfriend, Fran. We spent a lot of time talking about our homes, families, and past experiences. He was Catholic like me, but we were both backsliders from strict church attendance and following all the rules. Tom was a second- or third-generation Italian, and he talked a lot with his hands. What I liked most about Tom was his sense of humor. He always found something funny even when he was the victim of a joke, mishap, or prank. I remember on one training exercise he stepped into what appeared to be a small water-filled ditch, but it was actually a deep foxhole. He sunk into the cold water and muck damn near up to his neck. We pulled him out and all laughed at his predicament. Even though he and his gear were a big mess, he also laughed like hell after a few minutes. But, aside from enjoying a prank or joke on others or himself, Tom was also a good buddy to have in a brawl. Several times we got involved in bar melees, and he proved a fearless fighter, unafraid of even the biggest guy in the room. Tom was easygoing and always ready to try something new or plow into a new adventure.

Throughout training we continued to see less than encouraging newsreels about battles, massacres, and destruction all over Europe and Asia. It looked as though those places were burning up, and the Germans and Japanese seemed the chief culprits. President Roosevelt continued to mention peace and treaties, but it slowly became apparent to Tom and me that we would eventually get into a war somewhere. Many rumors began flying around about our company being deployed to England or Hawaii, but no one really knew, and as privates we realized we would be the last to know. On a bright chilly fall morning, our platoon formation was fronted by our company commander. He ordered us to parade rest and then read an order that called for our deployment in several weeks to a secret overseas destination. He concluded by telling us we would be granted a one-week leave before deployment. For the next few days, the mess hall and barracks chatter was all abuzz about our "secret" destination. Every possible place was guessed, but the running joke was our next stop would not be a vacation place.

My weeklong leave back home was outstanding, seeing Catherine, friends, and family. However, the hours and days raced by, and we soon admitted an uncertain future given my upcoming deployment. We happily shared our young married life and dreams though a cloud seemed to shade our plans for the happily-ever-after part. All in all, it was a bittersweet week. While Catherine and I kidded around a lot, and her mother continued to insist I eat more, the air of uncertainty grew. We simply did not know the future and realized it was hard to seriously plan anything. Everything was up in the air because I had no idea where I was heading or how long I would be gone. We promised each other our love forever, no matter what the future might hold. It was decided Catherine would stay home with her folks until my overseas duty ended. We assured each other that we would stay in touch by mail, telegrams, and phone calls. This farewell was tougher than our earlier brief separations. While Elwood, Mr. Williams, and the other men offered best wishes and joked about my upcoming year in Hawaii, it was tougher saying goodbye to the women. Catherine's sisters, Mrs. Williams, and Martha tightly hugged me and cried as I tried to reassure them not to worry. Finally, at the train station, I kissed Catherine one last time and boarded the train. I slumped into my seat feeling absolutely miserable. Outside the window Catherine was standing there showing a brave smile while tears ran down her rosy cheeks. She blew kisses, gave a slow wave, and then disappeared.

The train was a troop train. As we headed south into North Carolina, more men hopped on board at towns and little villages. The rail car was filled with laughter and loud conversations, but as the miles passed by, things quieted down. Then someone said we were in Georgia, and I realized this was probably not the best way to England or Europe. In September, Britain, France, Australia, and a few other countries declared war on Hitler, and everyone assumed we would be crossing the Atlantic. The chatter on board guessed many places as our destination, which convinced me no one really knew except the general or commander in charge. As we click-clacked along the rails, the train added more passenger cars in several cities. Peering out the window and looking forward and backward, our train resembled a long gray snake spitting out black clouds. I walked through six or seven cars before I found Tom, and it was mighty good to see my buddy. We traded seats with other fellows and lugged our bags to our new location. The train never stopped for very long except at one station in the middle of the night. There, a lot of hollering and cussing woke everyone up. Within an hour, word spread about two boys who decided to go over the hill by jumping off the train. They were caught and got military police (MP) seatmates for the rest of the trip. I think we ate, slept, and smoked our way to Atlanta for the two or three days it took to get there. They let us off the train just long enough to drop off postcards, buy fresh smokes or snacks, and use the bathrooms.

Next, we dragged our gear to a new waiting train, got seated, counted, and were immediately called to attention. Everybody hopped up like rabbits when a captain appeared and told everyone to sit back down and relax. He had our orders and told us we were heading to California where we'd be shipped out somewhere across the Pacific Ocean. He told us we'd get our next orders once we got to the West Coast. The talk now turned to possible war with Japan. For the next week or so, we rumbled westward over mountains, past vast empty plains and field upon field of corn and wheat, and through huge deserts and little towns and cities. We stopped every day or so, and everyone was allowed time to get off, stretch, send mail, or buy snacks. Somehow at every stop Tom managed to find a place to buy a pint or two of whiskey. Of course, booze was not allowed on the troop train, but it didn't matter to Tom. He enjoyed a swig or two, but I had lost my appetite for the stuff as it easily upset my stomach. While Tom enjoyed his liquor, I enjoyed my smokes. With or without his Canadian Club, Tom was a slaphappy kind of guy, and he kept our spirits up with his jokes and pranks. I worried about our uncertain destination, but Tom acted as though he was on holiday. He was a helluva boost to me on days when I got the blues worrying about my young wife and things back home.

In early October 1941, we arrived at Angel Island in California. It was great to finally get a decent shower and fresh chow and get off the train. We spent a few days getting shots, undergoing physical training, getting more gear, and filling out forms. Since leaving home, I had managed to send Kakie a postcard or letter almost every day, but my supply of stamps had run out. Finally, we got orders to board the SS *President Cleveland*, an old luxury liner from the 1920s. It had been converted into a troop ship and renamed USS *Tasker H. Bliss*. We still didn't know where we were heading, but a sergeant finally told us our orders and destination would be announced once we got aboard and out to sea. I became desperate for a postcard or stamp to let Catherine know what I knew about our mission. Nobody had stamps to sell or trade. When I told Tom, he laughed and pulled from his knapsack a handful of penny postcards.

Best I can recall, it was the first or second week of October when we were trucked down to the docks and boarded the big gray troop ship that became our home for the next month. A sailor on board told me the ship had been built at the Newport News Shipyard, which is just across the James River from Portsmouth ... small world. The ship was certainly no longer a luxury liner. Hammocks and bunks were crammed together on several decks, and in every corner topside, military gear was lashed down. Even at a dock with calm water, the ship rocked back and forth like a bar of soap in a bathtub. Once the ship hit open waters and bobbed around a few hours, the vomiting began. I had never seen so much puking in my whole life. The poor guys were throwing up and going goofy everywhere. Luckily, rough waters didn't bother me, and I never got seasick. However, the unrelenting sight, smell, and sound of guys groaning to puke or dry heave nearly made me ill a few times. Several unlucky crewmembers spent a lot of time mopping and rinsing the decks and stairways the entire trip. It was sickening. Day after day there was vomit on the stairways, decks, and mess area. One had to be careful not to slip or slid in the mess. I felt sorry for the poor saps with the weak stomachs.

Finally, after a few days out in the ocean, we were told our official orders directed us to the Philippine Islands. I did not know much about the Philippines except it became a US territory after the Spanish American War. Our sergeant had been there and called it the "pearl of the Orient." He said it was filled with palm trees, beautiful beaches, mountains, jungles, and small, friendly brown people. He told us the climate was tropical, and the islands had been his favorite overseas assignment. We stopped in Hawaii and Guam for fuel and supplies, but no one was allowed to get off the ship. During our sea days, we had daily physical training and classes about what to expect in the Philippines. At night our ship began running dark for safety reasons. This meant few lights were allowed on the decks, and the lights below were dimmed. During the days and evenings when the weather was good, Tom and I spent our free time with others lying on the deck. There we shot the bull, played cards, and occasionally shot craps. Even on hot days the deck became a better place than the stinky passageway, stairways, and ladders glistening with fresh puke. Our sleeping area was constantly hot because there was little movement of fresh air.

Near the end of October, we arrived in Manila, and it was hot and humid. I was surprised by the beauty of the large city and its harbor. All the buildings were gleaming white, and the water colors were beautiful blues and greens. After gathering up our gear and marching off the boat, we were allowed an hour's free time. The first thing I did was telegram Catherine. I revealed I was in the Philippine Islands, everything was good, and I missed and loved her. Telegrams were expensive, so I didn't write too much, knowing for just a few pennies I could send her a longer letter. Before our hour break was over, I remember buying a bottled soda while smoking a cigarette and thinking about my voyage halfway across the world to this exotic place. My first impressions were good although I still wished I was back home on Lansing Avenue. I felt the Philippines would be an interesting experience given the different people, smells, sounds, scenery, and languages it offered. Things I had never experienced before were awaiting me. Then a loud whistle roused me from my thoughts about this new place, and I remembered the Japanese threat was the real reason for our presence.

After a dusty ride, we arrived at Clark Field, which was a short distance from Manila. This was the largest US Army Air Corps base in the Philippines where the huge B-17 bombers, smaller P-40 fighters, and a variety of other older aircraft were stationed. Tom and I were still assigned to the 803rd Aviation Engineer Battalion, and our job would involve keeping the runways clear and usable for the flyboys. Naturally, being a GI (government issue) grunt, we also had other duties, such as kitchen police (KP) and guard duty. Even though Clark was a large base, the increase in so many new soldiers and airmen meant the existing barracks didn't provide enough sleeping spaces. They couldn't build them fast enough to keep pace with all the new personnel arriving. Consequently, Tom and I, along with others, were assigned to live in a large canvas squad tent that had bunk space for a dozen. Each man got a bed and a foot locker to stow his gear. Little wooden sheds were nearby for showering and shaving, and large outhouse structures became our bathrooms. When things got buggy, we could seal up our tent, but this made our space hot. It quickly became a constant battle to keep the flies, mosquitoes, spiders, and gnats out of our tent. When the wind shifted or the bugs weren't too bad, we left the sides open to catch any breezes.

Tom and I were teamed up with two boys from New Mexico to form a work squad. Steve and Red were good fellows, and we all hit it off from the get-go. Soon we were racing around the runways in our little truck doing our aviation engineering jobs and keeping things clean and clear for our pilots and their planes. Every day there were dozens of training flights so we were kept busy. At night after chow, I wrote Catherine to tell her about my job and the new things I was seeing and experiencing. We got plenty to eat, especially on Thanksgiving Day 1941. A large tent housed an enlisted club, and there a fellow could enjoy a few beers or shots of hard liquor, play cards and ping pong, listen to a radio broadcast, get a donut, or simply use the free stationery to write letters home. I listened to a few radio news reports, and things were looking bad. We were at war in Europe, and the Japanese were overrunning many of their neighbors with massive troop invasions and air attacks. When I began getting mail from Catherine every few days, the appearance of her letter and slight scent of perfume became the highlight of my day. I bundled her letters and, until new ones arrived, read and reread the old ones.

About this time I also started getting a little more serious about my religion. I guess the possibility of war scared me. Although I had received Catholic schooling, I abandoned the church and had gotten damn close to being a jailbird a few times during my younger rough-and-rowdy days. I remembered the teachings about the Lord having mercy on sinners, and I knew I was a sinner, so I started praying a little every night. I prayed to be a better Christian and begged God to help me if war came. I also prayed that the Lord help my buddies and keep Catherine and family safe during these frightening times. On an especially hot and sunny Sunday, I made my first confession in a very long time and received Holy Communion. I was scared of what might happen if the Japanese followed through on their threats about taking over the Philippines and figured getting a little closer to the Lord was a good thing. Tom was also born and raised Catholic and attended a few masses with me. However, Tom told me he didn't need all the church stuff since he and God had daily conversations, and he felt God knew what was in his heart. A chaplain gave me a rosary, and I started using it.

With Tom it was easy to find ways to goof off when he got breaks from work. Although we were told not to wander off base, we did anyway. We enjoyed exploring the nearby jungles and were amazed by the brightly colored wildlife and plants. Weird-looking lizards, trees, plants, birds, and snakes, along with all the crawling and flying insects, were interesting. One day we were walking along a path and met up with several small black men and a boy. They were as surprised as we were, and while the men only stood about four feet tall, their nakedness and tall bows immediately got our attention. Fortunately, their toothless grins, friendly gestures, and the broken English of the little boy made our encounter peaceful. They were members of the Negrito tribe, and we found out later that some of their number were headhunters. On a future encounter with the same men, they demonstrated their skills by shooting a goofy-looking bird far up in a tree. They were experts with their long bows. At my request, they allowed me a try. The bow must have had a pull of a hundred pounds, and my shot at a lizard was a big miss. They giggled, and after several other meetings, they told us they very much liked Americans, hated the Japanese, and were worried about war coming to their home. These Negrito tribesmen were not as primitive as those in the mountains who still practiced some old ways, including headhunting, idol worship, and tribal war. One day Tom and I ventured a few hours up into the hills and encountered several natives who led us to their small barrio. Inside a thatched hut, they proudly showed us several items that in the dim light looked like shriveled baseballs. Looking closer, they we clearly shrunken heads with strands of hair and tiny bulging eyes. I found handling one of the gruesome, sewn-together skins was a spooky experience. These men were not Negritos. One spoke a fair amount of English and said the heads were considered battle trophies. Over the next few weeks, Tom and I engaged several other Filipinos in the bush. They were eager to learn about us and America, and we gladly listened as they taught us a little about their jungle world and way of life. The men we encountered were usually friendly and helpful in showing us the plants and animals to avoid and the way to best use a machete to get through dense underbrush. They also suggested ways to avoid poisonous snakes, spiders, and leeches. We were curious to learn their skills, never realizing the things we were shown would prove important in the coming months.

In addition to our regular army duties, we were required to attend training sessions that covered everything from malaria to contracting syphilis from the local whores. Official army slide presentations about tropical living gave us practical tips on how to avoid mosquitoes, flies, sunburn, and contaminated drinking water. We were lectured on the Philippine and Japanese cultures and people. The frequent newsreels revealed the brutality used by the Japanese military against the regular folks in China and other places they had overrun. Over in Europe, it appeared Hitler and Mussolini were winning at every turn. While Tom and some of the other boys joked about the small size of the Japanese soldiers, I wasn't so sure. In the past I had taken a lot of beatings from guys smaller than me, and I felt these small men were probably tough sons of bitches despite their size. But I wasn't an infantry grunt and didn't expect to be one. I was content cleaning and patching the airfields with Tom, Red, and Steve. Even in November the climate and humidity remained stifling, and I sweated heavily along with my buddies. Back home I knew the weather had cooled, but here if you weren't covered with perspiration, you were drenched by monsoon rain. Naturally, with the heat and rain came legions of bugs. It was difficult to sit down or stand around without attracting a variety of biting and chewing bugs. We were told to especially avoid and swat the mosquitoes because they carried malaria. The bug ointments we were issued and the netting over our bunks didn't totally keep the nasty insects away.

On one weekend pass, Tom and I got a chance to visit Manila. We rode a little train that ran from the base to the city. While we were sitting and enjoying the scenery, this little old lady worked her way down the aisle. She was lugging a basket of fruit and eggs and selling items to passengers as we rolled down the tracks. When she got to us, Tom rummaged through her basket and pulled out two duck eggs. He was hungry and wanted to buy what he thought were hard-boiled eggs. He handed her a few centavos, peeled the shell away, and bit into the first egg. To his surprise, and my amusement, he spit out a mouthful of dead duck and black juice. It was disgusting and stinky. Well, Tom jumped up and hollered for the old woman to come back. Then he raised hell, holding a handful of duck and juices for the woman to see and demanding a refund. The old woman smiled and shook her skinny finger directly at Tom's nose. In pretty good English, she explained that the egg with the duck embryo was a delicacy and a healthy thing to eat because it was full of calcium. Needless to say, Tom did not get his money back. He grumbled for a few minutes and then, to my surprise, eyed the remaining uneaten egg. I watched as he peeled and slowly chewed the whole thing. Although his face twisted, and he looked ready to wretch, Tom grinned and told me it was pretty tasty after all. Later we found out the old lady was right. The popular duck egg was called *balut* and considered a healthy snack.

In Manila we wandered around and went into a few shops, old buildings, and churches. It was nice how many people smiled and treated us American soldiers with respect. Local policemen and members of the Philippine Constabulary and Filipino Scouts were courteous, and some even saluted. The city was beautiful with all its white buildings and tropical parks. There were many street vendors selling delicate lace, pearl jewelry, bamboo trinkets, snacks, silk scarves, carved ivory, bone figurines, Coca-Cola, and cheap knickknacks. I bought Catherine a pearl bracelet and necklace set. It came in a pretty case, and I intended to ship it to her after the weekend. There were many other GIs roaming the streets, some arm in arm with their new Filipino girlfriends. Laughter drifted in and out of the bars and eating joints and livened up the streets. Aside from the old hookers, many of the younger local girls were quite beautiful. Their dark hair, slim bodies, and deep brown eyes made them appealing. From the time we landed, the army constantly warned us of venereal diseases in the islands, and I decided to enjoy looking but not touch. Since we were lectured and shown movies with horrible images of male private parts destroyed by syphilis, I decided against messing around with any of the women. Things were so bad that MPs were stationed outside some cathouses. There they directed men to little nearby tents manned with medics and orderlies. The army called these places "pro stations," and it was the place soldiers who frequented whorehouses had to register, get cleaned up, and get shots or exams. In addition to the prostitutes in Manila, there were many in and around Clark Field, Fort Stotsenburg, and the nearby barrios. I remember pulling garbage duty and seeing many sick guys in a field hospital that, I was told, was filled with victims of venereal diseases.

At breakfast mess, on the morning of December 8, 1941, news spread quickly about Pearl Harbor. Word quickly got around that the massive navy base in Hawaii had been destroyed, many men killed or wounded, and a good portion of our fleet sunk. Some said Hawaii had been invaded by Jap soldiers and a Japanese fleet was steaming eastward set to attack California. There were no radio broadcasts in the dining area, so the reliable accounts were coming from orderlies and radio shack men who had heard the reports over shortwave or repeated by officers. There were many other reports flying around, but it seemed certain the Japanese had attacked a US military base, and we assumed this meant we were at war with the Japanese. It was called a sneak attack and reminded me of the many sucker punches I took as a kid when I underestimated the other guy. Many men were saying, "We are now in it," and nobody seemed very surprised. I remember looking around the mess hall and seeing some groups excitedly chattering and others finishing their chow in silence. I was apprehensive but trusted the army and air corps could handle most anything the Japs threw our way. Things were a little quieter than normal as our crew shoved off to work. A few minutes into our normal duties, our platoon sergeant raced toward our truck in his jeep. He ordered we double-time to get the runways policed up, as extra training takeoffs and landings had been scheduled. As he hammered down the accelerator, he abruptly slammed the brakes and hollered back at us that the news had just come in: President Roosevelt was officially declaring war on Japan.

It was about noon, and we were busily filling and patching potholes when we heard the low roar of planes overhead. The sound grew deafening, and I thought it was some B-17s coming in to land. Most of our B-17s were lined up nearby on a main runway, so we assumed this was an additional group coming in to beef up our bomber squadron. We couldn't see anything through the thin clouds, as the planes were mile high, but the sound was getting louder by the second. Then we heard the first explosions and saw giant red fireballs and dark smoke flashing all around our parked bombers. Quickly, it was obvious we were under attack. We flopped flat to the ground and could clearly see the bombs tearing the hell out of our aircraft, runways, and buildings. I cannot recall any of our fighters or bombers getting off the ground, and they were parked like sitting ducks and getting destroyed by the intense and unrelenting bombs raining down. After a few minutes, we ran into a small grove of bushes and watched the action. Our antiaircraft guns finally came to life and were shooting every which way, but I didn't see any Jap planes crashing.

Of course, we were all scared to death, and I distinctly remember Tom next to me mumbling a "Hail Mary" while in the same breath cursing the Japs as bastards. As Red, Steve, and I snatched palm fronds to hide ourselves, I was so terrified I almost pissed myself. In the first moments of that awful attack, I realized someone was doing their damnedest to kill me, and I wasn't the tough guy I imagined. So, there we were: four guys groveling in the sand and dirt, armed with only shovels and rakes and hiding from all hell blasting down from the skies. Some of the bombs were so close I could hear their whistling as they descended and feel the ground shake from their concussions. The burning smell of gunpowder combined with blasted dirt was suffocating. Shrapnel was flying overhead and shredding trees while setting fires to the fields of cogon grass. Big chunks of dirt were popping up all over the place as bomb fragments and B-17 pieces flew everywhere. Some of the bombs contained phosphorous, which is a white-hot material that burns through anything. I witnessed, on this first day of war, a fellow running nearby and screaming his head off. He was on fire and likely hit by a piece of phosphorous. His screaming lasted a few minutes, and then he fell to the ground and didn't holler anymore. We couldn't help him, as we were pinned down, and shovels and rakes were certainly no match for the big bombers high above.

After what seemed a long time, the bombers ended their barrage and flew away. I popped up with the other boys and couldn't believe the destruction. The paved runways were full of big holes, and all of the planes I could see were torn up or burning. Buildings were smashed and blazing. Smoke was heavy in the air, and sirens blended in with human screams to complete the nightmarish scene. There was a lot of confusion as jeeps, trucks, and ambulances raced around retrieving the injured. Fire engines attacked the roaring fires all over the base. The blazes continued for hours. We got to our truck and decided to head back to headquarters and find out what we should or could do to help. This attack was our Pearl Harbor, and at the time I honestly felt our commanders didn't know it was coming since our aircraft remained on the ground, and few if any got off the ground. It was a sucker punch from the enemy, and we took it in the gut. Back at our headquarters, sergeants and officers were yelling and ordering their squads and companies to assemble. Despite the fire and destruction, some order returned, and we were directed to get back to the runways and "bust a gut" to get the junk off the airstrip and fill the holes. Speeding back, we passed a grassy area where dead soldiers were covered and lined up in rows. We also saw bloodied men staggering and others on stretchers being rushed to aid stations.

We began work immediately and were working our butts off when we heard the overhead growling again. This time nobody doubted it was another attack by the Jap bombers. We rushed into a field of sugarcane and planted ourselves in the furrows between the rows. Using helmets and shovels, Tom and I frantically did our best to bury ourselves. Steve and Red found a foxhole on the edge of the field and were able to bend down and get their heads below ground. This time the bombs were falling closer to us. After the shrill whining sound, the ground below shuttered as the bombs smashed into the earth. Big clumps of dirt and sugarcane plants were flying in all directions. Lying in the dirt and sucking in mouthfuls of dust, I wondered what could possibly be left to bomb and why I didn't hear any antiaircraft gunfire. While the bombers were going like gangbusters, Tom and I glanced nervously at each other a few times. When the bombing finally ended, we pulled ourselves out of the dirt covered in dust, which had turned to a muddy glaze from our sweat. At this point nobody gave a damn, as we were happy to have survived the second bombing of the day. A quarter-ton truck sped up to our pickup, and a corporal called us over. He gave each of us a rifle and boxes of shells and told us to defend ourselves if enemy infantry or paratroopers attacked. The guns were old Springfield and Enfield models, possibly from the last war, and none of the rifles were automatics. It was slightly reassuring to have something to fight with other than garden tools. We loaded our guns, stuffed our pockets with extra bullets, and resumed clearing the airfields.

On our run in to get some chow, we encountered a fellow roaming around alone. We stopped and saw his arm was bleeding badly, and he was talking crazy. Tom used some rags to stop the bleeding; then we loaded him in the truck and sped off to a hospital tent. We lingered at the aid station until a medic came out and told us the boy was suffering from shock and a shrapnel wound but should make it. That day our chow was canned stuff called K rations, which became our steady diet since the mess kitchen had been shut down due to bombing damage. We returned to work, and within a few minutes, we heard a different sound coming through the clouds. It was a noise different from the low groan of the bombers. These were Jap fighter planes called zeros, and they made a screaming sound and flew lower. Their shrill buzzing as they swooped out of the sky reminded me of a giant swarm of angry wasps. The small and fast fighter planes quickly dived down in all directions and toward us. Because they were flying low, it was easy to see the big red balls on the fuselages, flashes from their guns, and the pilots' faces. Man, did we run from those spraying bullets. Those sons of bitches were busy gunning down people and anything else not already blown up. Unlike the big planes, these suckers could clearly see their targets and aim precisely at whatever they wanted to shoot.

As we ran for cover, fresh pieces of dirt from exploding bullets followed us until the four of us dove into a ditch full of green muck. This hiding place was a hole filled with slimy green water and surrounded by tall weeds, but nobody cared. The zeros were swooping down in waves, and as I squirmed around to get a better look, I saw a pilot grinning as he buzzed overhead blasting the hell out of everything. Angry, I started shooting at one plane as it blasted by our position, and Tom damn near knocked my head off and told me to stop. He screamed that our bullets couldn't hit the fast-moving fighter, and we were only calling attention to our location. Tom was right. I was damn mad and felt the need to fight back or do something. Red and Steve were also firing at the planes, but the pop, pop, pop of their carbines was pitiful compared to the roar of the automatic guns firing hundreds of rounds. We huddled in the mud for a long time, trying to be invisible until the zeros stopped their strafing and sped away. Cautiously we climbed out of the ditch and stumbled to our truck, which was splattered with mud, pieces of dirt, and a few bullet holes. All of us were filthy, angry, and frustrated, having caught so much hell and unable to fight back. None of us had ever experienced a situation where other men were trying to kill us, and it was a bad feeling. As kids and young men, we all had fistfights and wrestled around, but other than a bloody or broken nose, nobody was ever trying to kill. While we field-stripped and cleaned our filthy rifles, Red commented that our small-caliber guns were no match for the attacking planes, and we should get ourselves a machine gun or automatic for the next fight. Everybody agreed.

Soon we were back cleaning debris from the runway and surveying the burning hangars, aircraft, and fires all over Clark and off into the nearby barrios and hills. It looked as though none of our planes had escaped damage, but men were all over the planes with fire hoses, and some were stripping off undamaged parts. Along one field far away from any hangar, we spotted an unmanned jeep with a mounted gun. We raced up, looked around, and since nobody was nearby, we decided to requisition the gun for our truck. We quickly unbolted the gun mount and jerry-rigged it to our vehicle. The gun was a 30-caliber model and seemed in pretty good shape. The heavier gun strapped to our truck boosted our confidence that we might have a better way to defend ourselves and fight back.

During the afternoon of December 8, we continued to rush around patching the runways and doing our best to push blown-up junk off the airstrips. We kept watching and listening for more air attacks, but none came. In the distance, at the end of a runway, we spotted a crowd of kids gathered around a burning hulk. Checking it out, we discovered a dozen or so Filipino boys dancing around a crashed and burning Japanese fighter. It was an enemy plane that our ack-ack guns had knocked down and the only Jap wreck we had seen all day. Moving closer, we saw the canopy of the plane had been ripped off, and the upper part of the pilot's body was visible but horribly mangled and still burning. An arm and the back half of his head were missing. Several boys were using sticks to poke his bubbling flesh. The kids, probably eight or ten years old, were laughing up a storm. It was a gruesome sight, and the burning corpse gave off an ungodly smell. This was the first dead Jap I had seen, and I didn't feel one bit sorry for him. While I knew he had a family like the rest of us, he and his pals had attacked us without warning for reasons I didn't fully understand. On this first day of war, many of our men had been injured and killed, so I was very angry. Looking around the wreckage, I noticed a piece of the plane had broken off, and a manufacturer's plate was still intact and visible. It read "Curtis Wright and Company." We realized in an instant that some parts of this damn plane had been built in the United States. After a few more minutes, we drove off and left the boys to their fun.

The first day of our war was coming to an end, but fires with streams of black-and-white smoke were still rising in all directions. The sunset was an orange glow reflecting the fire. The light early evening breeze carried a heavy smell of burning oil and wood in the air. The four of us were filthy and exhausted but lucky to have escaped without any injuries. As we headed toward our billeting area, we noticed more rows of covered bodies and several injured men milling around the medic tents. These poor suckers were the first American casualties in the Philippines, just a day after the surprise attack on Pearl Harbor. I guessed some of these guys were near me at breakfast and probably jabbering about their wives, girlfriends, and home. The quickness between life and death scared the hell out of me, and I realized my buddies and

I could have been casualties as easily as these poor guys. After getting some food and washing up, we sat around and talked about all we had seen and what might be coming next. At our evening formation, our platoon sergeant told us our company had been ordered to nearby Del Carmen Field. He also read off the names of guys in our outfit who had been killed or injured and asked us to keep them in our prayers.

Somehow our squad tent survived the bombs, and except for a few extra layers of dust, it seemed a safe place from all the hell we had endured. Like the others I stretched out on my cot and filled the air with cigarette smoke. A few guys tried to tell jokes or pass on fresh rumors, but it was mostly quiet. Sleep was really hard, and the shock of bombing and grisly images kept floating around in my head. I tried to think about Catherine and getting home safe from all this mess, but it all now seemed a million miles away. Finally, the steady sound of Tom's snoring settled my racing thoughts, and I feel asleep.

War Begins -
Retreat to Bataan

Early on the second morning of the war, we grabbed bis-
cuits and coffee before jumping into the bed of a half-ton
truck. Each of us lugged our duffel bags and carbines. We
also hauled aboard our recently swiped 30-caliber and its
ammo. In all the morning confusion, our platoon sergeant
didn't notice or give a hoot that we were carrying off an un-
assigned machine gun. The run to Del Carmen was a short,
bumpy ride due to serious potholes from the previous day's
bombings. Along the roads we passed hundreds of civilians
walking, cycling, or riding in buses to get away from Clark
Field. Many were carrying bags and boxes and even pieces
of furniture. The pace of activity was frantic, and people
were shouting at each other and herding their children to
move faster.

Del Carmen was a smaller airfield that maintained P-35s and
other older aircraft. Along with Clark, it had been hit hard
the first day of war, and the Japs left much of the base a

leveled and smoldering mess. As we approached the field, it was obvious many of the planes were smashed. Once we threw our gear into the billeting area, our squad was quickly issued a small truck and a bag of tools to resume our normal duties. The first thing we did was secure our automatic gun to the truck's bed. We used ropes to tie it down and packed sandbags around its base to make sure it was stable. Tom found a tin of heavy grease, and we slathered the moving parts of the 30-caliber to ensure its smooth operation. None of us had any formal training on its use, but we figured a gun was a gun, and loading, aiming, and firing would be easy enough. After the gun was all set, we congratulated ourselves on having a new weapon to knock down a few zeros. In hindsight, despite the terrible attack of the previous day, the four of us were recalling old war movies and thought our mounted gun might make us heroes.

Close to lunchtime we heard the deep growl of the big bombers overhead and decided our gun couldn't reach the high flyers, so we moved our rig into a grove of bamboo. We burrowed ourselves into the ground using our folding shovels and waited. The whistling of the descending bombs, explosions of light and fire, and shaking of the ground around us came in waves. The shrapnel whizzing overhead slicing up the palm and bamboo trees was a reminder of the destructive force of the flying metal fragments. It was another steamy day, and it wasn't long before I found myself caked in dust, which dissolved into mud as I sweated profusely. The bombs started new fires and reignited old fires from the previous day. Buildings and aircraft not already smashed were blasted again. As I peeked from the ground, it looked as though there was little that the Japs hadn't destroyed, but their bombing continued.

When the Jap bombers flew away, we found our truck was okay and resumed our duties. Picking up junk from the runways and using tar and gravel to fill potholes, we did our best. Other crews were running around cleaning things up, and to our surprise several planes, including an old biplane, were able to land an hour or two after the bombing run.

Just as we were talking about lunch, the annoying scream of fighters filled our ears. We decided to move our rig to a field of tall pampas grass, which would give us some camouflage while allowing good visibility. Once positioned, Tom fired off a short volley, and the gun functioned perfectly, so we anxiously awaited a chance to shoot down an enemy fighter. As the bastards moved in closer, blasting everything, we noticed a zero heading our way. Tom excitedly jumped to man the gun while I stood by to feed him ammo. Finally, when the fighter swooped low toward our position, Tom fired, but after a dozen shots, the damn thing jammed. Since we had gotten the Japs' attention, he made a wide turn to execute a strafing run just for us. The gun was useless, and we only had seconds to escape, so we all scurried under the truck. As the pilot made a direct run overhead, the sound of bullets ripping up our rig became deafening. The truck vibrated from the firing, and I thought we were goners, especially if our fuel tank caught fire. After what seemed like an hour but was probably only seconds, the zero peeled off to find new targets. The attack lasted a while longer while we remained motionless. Pulling ourselves out from under what was left of our vehicle, it was a miracle everyone escaped injury. However, our pickup was a burning, destroyed heap. We stood silently in shock until Red joked that our "Willys" was a wreck but had shielded our butts. When he got home, he said he'd buy one since this one was so tough. We shouldered our firearms and shuffled away from the wrecked truck and useless 30-caliber toward our headquarters area.

Later in the evening, we related and embellished our experience with a few buddies until a sergeant first-class appeared out of nowhere. He quickly ordered the four of us to stand at attention. As we stood rigidly in line, he spent ten or fifteen minutes giving us a royal chewing out. As his face turned beet red, he screamed in each of our faces and showered us with his spit. First, he demanded to know how we expected to pay the army for the machine gun we swiped and the truck we got destroyed. Next, he wanted to know who the hell trained or ordered us to become artillery men. Finally, he questioned our parentage, intelligence, common sense, and masculinity, and he ended his tirade with a list of the sauciest expletives I had ever heard. A few minutes of silence followed as he stared daggers, and none of us dared a response. Then he shouted for us to get out of his sight, which we did. After a run to our tent, we stood around stunned until Tom quipped that maybe the army would fire us now, and we could go home. His comment was silly, but it broke the tension. I was embarrassed over the incident but also angry. While none of us had combat training and attempting John Wayne heroics was dumb, it was frustrating to take beatings and not fight back. I guess our squad was frustrated and wanted to let the Japs know we weren't pushovers.

For the next few days, the bombing and strafing raids became routine. We didn't bother using our rifles as the odds of hitting a racing zero were slim, so we simply found safe places to avoid the bombs and bullets. Talk at night centered on why we were taking it on the chin and not doing much to repel the air assaults. Everyone seemed to rate General Douglas McArthur as a decent enough leader with a good record, but why he and his generals couldn't stop the Japanese attacks remained a mystery. Rumors started floating about the 803rd becoming attached to the 31st or 57th Infantry since we had fewer air bases and usable runways left in the Philippines. Most disturbing, word was spreading that the Japs were landing massive armies on the north beaches and heading south toward us. Several days later, it was confirmed the Japanese had definitely landed huge forces to the north, and they were moving our way. We got orders shortly to move south from Del Carmen to a place called Bataan.

On the morning of our departure, we hopped aboard a truck and began our trip. The road was choked with cars, carts pulled by carabao, rickshaws, walking civilians, buses, motorbikes, bicycles, jalopies, and military vehicles all heading in the same direction. It looked like a poorly organized retreat, and the procession often stalled; when it moved, it was at a snail's pace. A handful of motorcycle-driving MPs weaved in and out, trying to keep things moving and resolving traffic accidents. The native people were also toting their possessions and herding goats and donkeys while keeping their children and older family members bunched together and heading in the right direction. Everyone had a bag or crate full of stuff. There were more Filipino soldiers moving south than American soldiers. Their military consisted of a constabulary, which was like the police; a regular army; and scouts, who many rated as their best troops. A fellow in our group said Bataan was seventy or eighty miles away and was a big peninsula of hills and mountains bounded by the South China Sea and Manila Bay. He was a college man and further related that the Bataan Peninsula might be a good defensive position since it was on high ground and near General MacArthur's headquarters.

After a few miles, Tom and I noticed the people walking were making better progress than our truck, so we decided to quit the truck and walk for a while. The road had stretches of hard packed earth, concrete, and asphalt with plenty of holes filled with mud. One good thing was the artesian wells that were alongside the road every few kilometers. These provided Tom and I with fresh canteens of cool water that helped keep us hydrated.

Walking through one of the larger barrios, a big Chinese man ran from his storefront and greeted us. In clear English he asked for our help for an hour, offering ten dollars to each of us for our service. He got our attention since ten dollars was more valuable than the local centavos or military funny money. He wanted us to guard his store against looters while he got his family and possessions loaded up and moving south out of harm's way. He promised to return in an hour or so to load up his store inventory and catch up with his family. It seemed a reasonable situation and a great deal for ten bucks. The convoy was still a slow-moving line stretching as far as the eye could see, so an hour or so wouldn't get us too far from our company. He pressed a ten-spot into our hands and rushed off.

His shop was a general store with a mishmash of products. There were shelves of canned goods, hunks of hanging dried fish and beef, and a display box full of pocketknives and pistols. Along the walls there were barrels of nails alongside crates of fresh vegetables and fruits. Tom and I liked the rack holding small bottles of liquor, packaged candies, cigarettes, and cigars. The place was clean, and things were arranged neatly. A few folks entered, but we firmly said, "Closed," and they went away. After a while surveying the store, we found two chairs and decided our guard duty would be easier if we sat at the front door. Also, this position would give us front-row seats of the parade slowly moving down the main road.

As I watched the crowds pass by, I felt sorry for the locals. They were rushing and obviously afraid of the approaching Japs. Such a shame these peaceful people were racing away from their villages and homes. I didn't understand everything about this new war but hoped President Roosevelt could work out a peace deal with the Japanese or at least give the military the means to send the enemy away. At the same time, I wondered, and frankly worried, how the folks back home would handle an invasion by Hitler on the East Coast. At some point I dozed off because a boom in the distance simultaneously roused Tom and I from our catnaps. The sound was surely the approaching Jap artillery getting closer, and since our Chinaman had not returned, we decided to rejoin the convoy. It had now been several hours since the Chinaman's promise to return. The line of evacuating civilians and military had thinned and actually sped up. As we prepared to leave, Tom pulled me back into the store and said he didn't think the owner would ever return and everything would be looted by the Japs, so we should help ourselves to a few things. I agreed as he swept many of the liquor bottles and cigars into his backpack. I loaded my sack with cigarettes and candy. Before leaving, we traded a knowing glance and placed our ten-spots near the cash register. We surely took our money's worth and knew the Japs couldn't do much with American money anyway.

Back on the main track, we resumed our walking and scrambled aboard a truck full of Filipino soldiers. The explosions were getting louder, and one of the boys on board said they were probably mortars. When our truck slowed to a stop, we bailed out in hopes of moving a little quicker to catch up with Steve and Red. After tromping along for a while, a jeep moved alongside and offered us a lift. We jumped into the back seats and introduced ourselves to the two lieutenants upfront. These officers were our age or younger and friendly, but I forget their names. Tom pulled out a few of his small Canadian Club bottles and offered them to everybody, but the young officers were busy jabbering and declined his offer. Tom took two and emptied them into his canteen, shook it with the water, and began to swallow healthy gulps. I ate a chocolate candy bar and then lit up a Pall Mall as I listened to the men upfront. Their conversation was interesting. One lieutenant was bitching about MacArthur's "strategic retreat order," saying the old man, Wainwright, and other generals had done a "shitty job" of getting the Philippines ready for war. The other agreed and called the strategic retreat stuff a lot of baloney. They also said the destruction of Clark and Del Carmen and most of our planes were unforgivable mistakes and reflected poor planning. During a pause in their chatting, Tom asked why everyone was going to Bataan.

The driver offered his understanding that the move would bring together Allied and Filipino forces to a strong, defensible position and future advantage over the Nips. The other junior officer agreed and added that a colonel in his outfit thought a huge fleet was on its way to deliver more troops and supplies. I didn't know if any of their information was accurate but sure hoped more troops, supplies, and aircraft were heading our way. The men upfront kept talking while Tom enjoyed his booze and I puffed away.

Our jeep moved along nicely, passing slower traffic and often weaving to the left or right to gain ground. After a half hour or so, a now-familiar awful noise filled our ears, which stopped all talking. The buzzing sound and a quick glance to our rear confirmed that a Jap fighter was bearing down on the long column of people and vehicles stretched behind us. Our driver veered sharply to the right into a rice paddy, and we bounded for cover alongside it. The lone plane zoomed down and laid a line of fire right down the middle of the road. The zero passed overhead in an instant but tore the hell out of everything in its path. Lying flat on the ground, we lingered, expecting the zero to make another run or other fighters to follow. This had been their pattern at Clark, Del Carmen, and Fort Stotsenberg, but as minutes passed, nothing happened except the screaming of the wounded and moans of grief over those killed. Many had jumped into ditches or steered their carts and vehicles off the road, avoiding the worst. Others bore the brunt of the aerial attack, and it was an awful spectacle. People were shot and bleeding while others were outright killed. Vehicles were consumed by fire and black smoke, and carabao-driven carts were overturned because the animal had been slaughtered. Their spilled cargo became a mess of debris. Confusion was everywhere. Along with others, we rushed to help people and reload their carts. Fortunately, a team of American medics was nearby, and they hustled into action using tourniquets and medicine to help the injured. We lingered awhile at the scene until the lieutenants told us there was little more we could do. Despite our efforts to get the jeep moving, it was junked because a few machine-gun shots tore through the hood and pierced the oil pan. Tom and I thanked the officers for the ride and bid them good luck as we rejoined the retreating procession that had slowly re-formed. As we walked, we discussed the inhumanity of a lone fighter pilot gunning down defenseless civilians and our good fortune in avoiding injury.

After a while, passing the roadside carnage, we convinced soldiers in a half-ton truck to squeeze out enough space on their bench for us to get a ride. They grudgingly agreed, and we had another ride. We slowly bumped our way farther south and finally passed the last of the strafing attack. Evidently the zero pilot had run out of ammunition at this spot. As a few men on board snoozed and others cursed the Japs. I simply stared at the passing countryside of green grass fields, rice paddies, and stands of palm and bamboo trees, all the while thinking about the terrible things I had seen in the last few days. Finally, late in the afternoon, we reached Hermosa where many Americans had stopped to spend the night. Scouting around, we found some of our 803rd buddies and related our stint as guards for the Chinaman and the zero attack we had witnessed. They were far ahead of us and didn't witness or hear any of strafing run. Tom shared some of his Canadian Club, and I shared a few smokes as we searched out places to rest on the bare ground. Before darkness it was important to find a sleeping spot away from fire ant hills or muddy places full of mosquitoes. Despite using a blanket for cover, I was pestered all night by the bugs like everybody else.

The next morning, we hopped aboard another half-ton and continued our trip to Bataan. There was no canopy on this truck, and before long the blazing sun popped up and was cooking everybody and burning exposed patches of skin. A few quick downpours offered a little relief, and stops at roadside wells gave us a chance for a quick dousing and fresh canteens of water. But best of all there were no more zero encounters. As we slowly made our way, we passed through the towns of Orania, Balanga, and Orion and many barrios and small villages where children and natives watched, waved, and smiled as our procession moved through. I noticed the changes in landscape as we gradually left the flatlands, began to encounter hilly country, and could see mountains in the misty distance. Conversations along the way were a mix of rumors, remembrances of home, bravado, and expectations of what we'd find in Bataan. Many were convinced a great force of fresh recruits and piles of new supplies were awaiting us upon arrival. Red and Steve were of the opinion that once we got things together at our new base, the Nips would be easily and swiftly whipped. Tom and I listened as he sipped his liquor and I smoked. As usual, I was convinced the only thing we knew was what we didn't know regarding the future of our deployment. Soon we began to hear thuds and booms in the distance, and someone said it was the noise of cannon fire or mortars, but nobody knew if it was from our guys or the Japs. Then we began passing bombed and wrecked vehicles. Some had been pushed down the embankment to keep the road clear, and others looked to be simply parked at the edge of the highway. The trucks and jeeps all had US markings but were not burning, and there were no bodies in sight; therefore, this destruction was not recent. The bullet holes and damage looked similar to what I'd seen from the zero assault the day before.

Soon we began to move into the mountains. The road became a twisted, narrowing passage, and the diesel trucks groaned as they ascended. Hairpin turns ground us to a routine of jerky stops and jolts forward as the truck gears kicked in and out. A few broken-down trucks had to ease to cliff sides to allow the one-way traffic to pass. In the middle of one switchback, we came upon a gruesome scene. A tractor trailer had somehow crashed into or been blown into a bulldozer. The wreck was still smoking, and the damage was the result of artillery or mortars and not bullets, as metal was twisted and parts blown all over the place. Worse, the body of the bulldozer driver was still in the open cab and impaled by an exhaust pipe rammed straight through his chest. The truck driver was dead, slumped over the steering wheel. This action was recent and may have been the bombing sounds we had heard earlier in the day. A cloud of black flies had descended on the dead men. Several medics were standing around but were unnecessary.

Our sergeant ordered Tom and me to dismount the truck and retrieve dog tags from the two dead men. We knew this was an important thing to do if we saw combat and any of our group got killed. In a remote place like this, a body might never be recovered, so dog tags were the only way to contact families. Tom rushed to the guy in the truck and easily retrieved his tags and wallet while I climbed the bulldozer. My job seemed impossible, and Tom joined me to help. We soon realized the exhaust pipe had jammed the fellow's tags deep into his chest. There was no way we could remove the man from the pipe, so I pushed my hand into his chest while Tom held back part of the gaping wound. My hand finally grabbed the two small metal tags, and I gently pulled them out. We also were able to move him enough to get his wallet. Needless to say, this was a sickening task. Tom and I were bloodied, but once we turned over the items and got cleaned up, I felt pleased to have helped ensure that the dead soldiers' people would get heartbreaking but proper notifications about their loved ones. The event again reminded me how uncertain things were, and the only way I could ever hope to survive was to completely trust in the Lord. After cleaning up and getting seated back in the truck bed, Tom and I sat quietly for a long time.

A day or two later, after twisting and turning through the hills and mountains, we finally reached Bataan. It was Christmas, and we once again got cots, tents, and a delicious holiday feast whipped up by our mess crew. For the next few days, things were quiet, and we enjoyed meals of turkey, mashed potatoes, cakes, good coffee, and even cranberry sauce. Not as great as the meals from Catherine's mother but nonetheless pretty darn good food. Somebody found a tree that barely resembled a Christmas fir, and we decorated it with stars and a variety of other odd homemade ornaments. At Mass we sang all the old Christmas carols, and after the service the priest gave us pieces of old-fashioned hard candy. After the scary experiences at Clark and Del Carmen, and while traveling north, things seemed much better at Bataan. For a few nights, I enjoyed good sleep and wonderful dreams of Kakie, family, and things back home. Naturally I got a little homesick, but steady work setting up our company area and defenses gave me little time to sit around and feel sorry for myself.

One morning, shortly after reaching Bataan, I decided to check out a small forest where some had seen deer. I hoped to kill one and give our cooks some fresh meat. The Philippine deer were smaller than the whitetails back home, but I figured a deer, monkey, or even wild hog would help our meat supply. With my carbine I hiked about a mile into the woods and found a comfortable spot underneath a tree to sit and wait. The area was quiet except for chattering birds and an occasional lizard running through nearby leaves. After an hour, when I was about to move, I distinctly heard something snorting but couldn't see anything. I lingered at my spot as the grunting got louder, and then, lo and behold, I saw a huge wild hog. It was getting closer and rooting around leaves and dirt just out of range, so I patiently waited. When the animal moved about twenty-five yards away and still wasn't looking my way, I quietly raised my rifle to take a shot. Wham, wham. I fired twice, and when the bullets crashed into the animal, it screamed and shook a little bit but didn't fall. Looking squarely at me, the wild boar charged. Man, oh man, was I scared seeing its size and thick yellow tusks. Just as I was about to shoot again, the hog collapsed to the ground. I waited a few minutes before approaching to ensure it was dead. Inspecting my kill, I was surprised at its massive size. It was muddy, foul smelling, and covered with thick hair. I had never shot such a large animal and realized it was too large for me to drag, so I decided to hike back and get some help. As I turned to leave, to my surprise another boar was charging. Quickly I clicked off two more rounds and dropped the second boar in its tracks. Either of these monsters could have torn me to pieces, and not knowing if they ran in packs, I decided to get the hell away in case any of their pals were nearby.

Racing back to the company area and remembering the route I had taken, I got Tom, Red, and several other fellows to follow me to the kill site. With poles and ropes, we secured the heavy boars and slowly made our way back to camp. A small crowd gathered and cheered as we plopped the hogs at the mess tent. The kitchen sergeant inspected the animals and declared we'd certainly be eating "high off the hog" for the next few days, and we did. The butchers provided us with fresh bacon, chops, and pork roasts for the next week. Although I had been an average marksman in basic training, this stunt made me a sudden hero. Men in the outfit and even a few officers praised my successful hunt. I went hunting a few more times before the Jap bombing and strafing began but never bagged any more game. Looking back, I honestly think killing those two boars was one of the best things I ever did while in the Philippines.

It was around New Year's 1942 when we began to hear distant enemy bombing, and word filtered down that MacArthur was cutting our food rations in half so supplies would last longer. Next, we were ordered to dig deeper foxholes and trenches near our tents and along our company perimeters. It was tiresome work spading through the clay and roots, but we knew the effort was necessary and might save our skins if and when the Japs attacked. Except for the peaceful week between Christmas and New Year's, we began to get bombed every damn day. The only difference from day to day became a question of how many attacks and the duration of the bombings. On a good day, they'd hit us once or twice, but on a bad day, the big bombers would unload six or eight times. During the attacks, the ground would bounce, and the sounds caused temporary deafness. Tom and I were trying to do our regular jobs but found ourselves jumping in and out of our foxholes and trenches when the bombing started. We joked that we had become hopping jackrabbits. What the Japs were doing was called carpet bombing, which meant they bombed extensively to cover an entire area like a carpet covering a floor. Many men were killed or injured during these bombing sessions by a concussion, flying shrapnel, or burning phosphorus. At the first sounds, it became important to get down low to avoid the bombs. But, even getting partially underground didn't guarantee safety because the white-hot phosphorus bounced around, and the concussion from a very close explosion could easily tear a man apart.

In addition to the high-flying bombers, they began bringing in waves of fighters that flew low enough to pick out buildings, equipment, and people running. These suckers sometimes came in just above the treetops and swooped lower in the open spaces to do their dirty work. The attacks extended beyond daylight, so we were getting hit at night too. Our medics were constantly on the move, getting the wounded to heavily camouflaged hospital tents. Their jobs were especially dangerous because they were retrieving victims in the midst of all the bombs and bullets. Our antiaircraft guns fired back, and the huge guns at Corregidor blasted away, but the Nip bombings became relentless and almost constant. The 803rd was a support unit, but we didn't have many airfields around Bataan and fewer planes so we were assigned other duties, such as truck driving and maintenance. Except for a few skirmishes, few in the 803rd had much combat training, but many were now carrying sidearms or rifles and wearing heavy metal helmets, including cooks, company clerks, mechanics, medics, and chaplains. While there were front lines of combat, it seemed everywhere was slowly becoming a front line. Having been in the Philippines less than two months, I found the incredible conditions had quickly gone downhill from peace to all-out war.

One assignment the 803rd got was keeping the mountain roads and bridges clear and passable. Tom, Red, Steve, and I did our best, dodging the bombardments, to remove the fallen rocks, shattered trees, and wrecked vehicles to ensure our supply lines remained open. The mountain roads were narrow and steep, and it didn't take much debris to block traffic. Maneuvering tanks, trucks, and earth-moving vehicles around the switchbacks was tough and dangerous work. More than once, we heard of drivers injured or killed when their rigs crashed down the embankments. We also helped to keep the few remaining airfields clear, although there were more seaplanes seen along the Bataan coast than ground aircraft.

Another job Tom and I were assigned was driving light trucks to and from Mariveles Point. The Point was a docking space for supply ships, a few subs, and small warships. It was our task to drive out of the mountains, race down to the wharf, pick up supplies, and rush back up the hills to make deliveries to the camps. At first, we thought this was a great job racing our trucks around the hairpin turns out of the mountains and then speeding down the long plain leading to the docks. However, the three-mile stretch of flatland between the last switchback and the coast soon became known as "suicide flats" because Jap snipers got stationed along our route. Even though our infantry did their best to get these guys, many were well hidden in the jungles and gave us fits. When a driver got shot, medics were sent out, and they also came under fire. Mechanics tried souping up our little rigs and attached armor plating, but that didn't help much. One guy painted "Indy Racer" on the side of his vehicle, and he came up with the best plan. As he charged down suicide flats, he would violently jerk his truck from left to right. This irregular zigzag pattern helped him evade the snipers but also produced a wild run, weaving on and off the main road while flying down the hill. Another concern became failing brakes. We heard of a few guys losing their brakes and splashing right into the water. Although a few men were killed or wounded, Tom and I were lucky and only got a few bullet holes in our truck's hood and fenders while we worked this crazy job. This assignment didn't last long because the Jap navy soon attacked our docking area and pretty much blockaded our shipping.

The relief fleet promised by the generals and predicted by many didn't come in the early weeks of the new year, and the food situation deteriorated. Lack of food became a sore point for everyone, causing arguments and even a few fistfights. It didn't take long for half rations to create hoarding, black marketing, and trading. Cigarettes, pocketknives, centavos, and even wristwatches were exchanged for cans of food or other items swiped from the food lockers. Things got so bad that armed guards were assigned to watch over the mess tents and places where food was stored. Although we were still getting fed, the portions were tiny, and asking for extra chow caused a lot of stress and anger.

To supplement our diet, Tom and I searched for berries and fruit between bombings, but since everyone else was doing the same thing, we didn't have much luck. Next we targeted big bugs and anything else slithering or hopping around. Roasted or boiled, some of these items were tasty while other items caused vomiting or diarrhea. The big beetles had a crunchy and salty taste, and the small snakes and lizards had a gamey flavor similar to the wild rabbit and possum I had eaten as a kid. Everyone realized the need for protein to maintain their energy, and some fellows were able to bag rats, monkeys, and stray dogs to eat. Although the odd concoctions Tom and I put together often caused us to gag, hold our noses, or throw up, it was the best we could do to combat our growling stomachs and gnawing hunger. In the coming weeks, unbeknownst to us, and before our surrender in April, our mess sergeants would slaughter, butcher, and serve us all the horses from the 26th Calvary. Also the horses' supply of oats became part of our morning meals. The cooks did a good job because I never realized any difference from our regular meat or morning gruel. By this time, I was so damn hungry and had eaten a lot of awful stuff that I became less picky about food. Our cigarette allocations were also reduced, and the nonsmokers made out well trading their smokes for K rations.

In the last weeks before we gave up, things went from bad to worse. The enemy slowed and then stopped the flow of mail to our base, which meant no more letters from Catherine or home. Sleep and rest became more difficult as the Japs increased the number of bombing and strafing runs at night. The loud explosions, bomb flashes of light, and orange-red tracer bullets were dangerous but also made it impossible to get a decent night's rest. Far off and well-hidden snipers became another constant threat. Occasional shots would zing by all hours of the day, directed at anyone walking around or standing out in the open. Some guys were injured and, I think, a few even killed by the snipers. A few times we were showered with leaflets from their planes. The messages were in English and stated we were losing the battle to hold Bataan and should surrender. The cards and flyers announced we'd get "honorable treatment" if we surrendered and announced a lot of other baloney. One piece even stated that no relief fleet or army was on its way to help us, and we'd all be slaughtered if we didn't give up the fight. This message eventually turned out to be true, but most everybody still held out hope that President Roosevelt and MacArthur would work out a rescue or peace deal to get us safely out of Bataan. Everybody considered the flyers a bunch of malarkey and eagerly gathered up the sheets to use as toilet paper. In addition to combat deaths and injuries, the number of able-bodied men was steadily declining because some guys were simply cracking up over the stress, and others were sent to hospital tents suffering from malaria.

By late February, the Japs had landed more troops and nearly surrounded all of our positions. While their men surely had plenty of food, ammo, and supplies, we were starving and running out of things left and right. Also, the number of men sick from beriberi, malaria, and dysentery was increasing, according to a medic buddy, and we were rapidly running out of medicine and medical supplies. The lack of adequate food and rest sapped my energy level, and even my normally upbeat partner was depressed and worn down at times. From stories we heard, our front lines were quickly shifting from position to position practically every day and slowly retreating as the Nips advanced. Our sergeant told us their daily bombings were getting more precise because their ground spotters were close enough to provide better coordinates on the location of our infantry and artillery.

The combination of hunger, constant bombings, heat, piss-poor rest, mosquitoes, fire ants, and torrential downpours was making everyone miserable. One day an orderly from our headquarters company told Tom and I that he was sure more men were dying from hunger and illnesses than combat injuries. A few buddies, including Tom and Steve, began talking about escaping Bataan before the Japs overran our positions. However, nobody had a clear idea where to run. A few wanted to get a boat and go to MacArthur's headquarters on Corregidor. They said it was a safe place with a bunch of big guns perched high above the water, and there were lots of caves and good hiding places. Others thought rushing to the jungles or a barrio far away from Bataan was a good plan. The idea of crossing the Bay of Manila full of Jap patrol boats or dashing off into the wilderness or a village, surely occupied by Nips, didn't make much sense to me. Somebody seemed to have a reasonable objection to all the pipe dreams, and such talk eventually drifted to more pleasant talk about loved ones, good food, and things back home. Some, especially Filipino soldiers, did begin to disappear from our ranks. It wasn't too surprising for the native soldiers because they were especially hated by the Japs, and in turn they loathed the invaders from the north. It was hard to fault anyone getting away from Bataan, even though it made one officially AWOL, because conditions were becoming lousier by the day. God only knows how the runaways fared.

Soon the 803rd, along with other support units, was attached to the 31st and 57th Infantries. Overnight, cooks, company clerks, mechanics, riggers, medics, maintenance men, and other noncombat troops became, more or less, infantry guys. Everyone became active, running around digging foxholes, lugging combat gear, and getting quick lessons on the use of carbines, automatics, grenades, and mortars. An infantry corporal told us that some of our hand grenades had slow fuses, which meant a Jap might have time to toss the damn thing back. I decided not to use the things unless a situation got desperate, but Tom loved them. When enemy troops got close a few times, Tom and Steve enjoyed slinging their grenades, as if they were baseballs, in the general direction of where Nips were suspected. Luckily, we never had any tossed back into our foxhole. Enemy soldiers landing all over the Bataan Peninsula soon made practically everywhere a front line. A captain gave us training on setting up a crossfire offense using machine guns if Jap soldiers broke through our defense and began overrunning our position. The idea was to set up at least two guns, with one directing fire to hit knees and legs and the other aimed at the attackers' torsos. The idea was to disable some and get others trying to rescue their buddies. One experienced frontline soldier told us his squad had mowed down dozens of Japs using this technique. I never got set up with this strategy.

One hellish afternoon, Tom and I were catching constant small-arms fire from every direction, and in between cursing the Japs and praying, I thought we were goners. Exhausted and expecting enemies to be standing over us at any second, the big guns on Corregidor opened up and blasted our perimeter. This action evidently knocked out a gang of nearby Nips because after the barrage, things got quiet for a while. I believe the timely and accurate blasts from the "Rock" saved our asses. From somewhere deep in his rucksack, Tom pulled out a pint of whiskey, and we celebrated our reprieve from the heavy gunfire. First a few neat swigs were exchanged, and then healthy mouthfuls were gulped. Although I had not tasted booze in months, I enjoyed getting a little stewed. After a half dozen more swallows, we began laughing like loons for no good reason. We answered the occasional shots fired our way by popping up out of our trench and blasting away in the general direction of where our enemy might be hiding. Our antics continued until nightfall when our tired bodies and quiet found us slumping in our hole and sleeping. The next morning, before the first wave of big bombers, we ventured out to look around our position hoping to find piles of slaughtered Japs, but instead we discovered our drunken gunfire had instead shattered and slaughtered a number of nearby palms, bushes, and trees. Despite the hangover, this incident was one of the last happy times Tom and I enjoyed in an increasingly grim situation.

As the Japs edged closer, they began using mortars and cannons to rip away at our defenses. Unlike us, they seemed to have an unlimited supply of ammo and blasted away hour after hour. Our situation was grave given the relentless aerial attacks, incoming ground fire, and our diminishing supply of food and ammunition. Along with my buddies, I felt increasingly trapped without any safe exit or the diminishing possibility of a rescue fleet. Deprived of sleep and decent chow, as well as living in a state of confusion and uncertainty, was stressing everyone out. More men were bugging out of Bataan for parts unknown while a few poor souls were losing their minds. I saw several grown men crying uncontrollably or running around naked, mumbling gibberish. I was having more frequent spells of splitting headaches and jitters, and I saw Tom, Steve, and Red also suffering from the stress. By late March, our defenses had all but collapsed, and weary Filipino and American combat soldiers were steadily retreating into our area. One ragged and wounded army sergeant from the front told a bunch of us the Jap high command was really pissed about our continued resistance. The Japanese conquest of the Bataan area wasn't following their battle plan, and they had pulled reinforcements in from Singapore, according to this combat veteran.

Everybody started whispering about surrender. Hopes of reinforcements or a rescue flotilla evaporated. Even though whipped and exhausted, we all hated the idea of surrender, but nobody in our group could think of any reasonable alternatives. Even our noncoms and officers weren't offering much hope and seemed caught up in the mayhem of those last days before we gave up the fight. A few fellows remembered the leaflet promises of honorable treatment, food, and clean clothes if we surrendered, and they believed the Nips would treat us fairly. One kid told us about something called the Geneva Convention rules of war, which required captured soldiers' humane treatment, but nobody knew if the Japs would honor those rules. I remembered the newsreels of how the Japs handled the civilians in China and wasn't so sure our treatment would be any better. The majority of guys at Bataan were Filipino regular army, scouts, or members of the constabulary and were bailing out of Bataan in large numbers. These men were good soldiers and pals, and in no way cowardly. Nobody could blame them because of the Japs' bitter hate for them. Our military police didn't even stop or question the Filipinos or anybody else now leaving the area. There was some talk of the Japs exchanging us for Jap prisoners we had captured, but it was hard to figure how many and where we had captured many of their soldiers. Red and Steve continued to favor taking off for the mountains or jungles, but Tom and I disagreed. We knew the Japs and their sympathizers were everywhere and, combined with the rough and unknown terrain, our chances of survival would be slim. Grudgingly, the four of us finally came to hope and believe that our large number would influence the terms of our surrender and get us decent treatment after surrendering.

Beat-up, dirty, hungry, sick, and near total exhaustion, we prepared for surrender when the orders filtered down. Few were surprised, and some even felt that a well-provisioned Japanese army could only improve the horrible conditions of our last few months. Some grumbled about Roosevelt and MacArthur abandoning us. In fact, it would be years before learning the president actually made the European part of the war a higher priority than the Pacific campaign in the Philippines. Along with my buddies, I thought it was all depressing, and I worried my homecoming and reunion with Kakie, friends, and family wasn't going to be any time soon. Orders were given to destroy our combat equipment, records, and supplies by fire or dismantling. A few men buried their automatic weapons and ammo in hopes of using them again, but most of us gave up our carbines and remaining cartridges. A few fellows carefully buried their wedding rings, watches, wallets, and money for later retrieval. Hospital personnel rigged huge red crosses to mark the hospital tents, and we heard that the medics and nurses were trying to use up or hide their remaining medicine and medical gear. A few days before our official surrender, the bombing and incoming gunfire stopped, and the new quiet was nice and also a little spooky. I was surprised at the tweets, croaks, and sounds of the creatures in the surrounding forests. I thought it was a miracle so many had survived the constant warfare and wondered if they were celebrating the sudden peace and quiet too.

On the morning of April 9, 1942, we were roused by Jap soldiers walking into our bivouac area. The first soldiers I saw were a sloppy bunch. Except for their officers, they were dressed in tattered and dirty uniforms, and their unshaven faces were as dirty as ours. These were their combat troops, and though I was surprised by their small size, they appeared to be a well-fed and fit bunch. On the other hand, some of their officers were in good-looking uniforms, sporting medals and fancy swords. The regular soldiers carried rifles with slender, extra-long bayonets, which stood taller than any of them. A few soldiers carried only sidearms or long bamboo poles.

It wasn't long before the officers barked orders, and the enlisted men bowed and grunted. Their interactions seemed funny, but no one dared laugh at their military customs or some of the other queer things they did during our first minutes of surrender. None of us knew their language and had no earthly idea what they were taking about or what was going to happen next. A few of their guards surprisingly knew and offered the word *hello* to some, and a few offered cigarettes to their captives. However, within a short period of time, the guards began to direct and shove everyone into groups. Tom, Steve, Red, and I were bunched together with several dozen other men. For no apparent reason, the Japs with sticks walked around and started whacking soldiers in the head. They were especially drawn to the Filipinos and bloodied those poor men with repeated blows to their heads. Then we were lined up, and guards came along to take our possessions. Rings, watches, wallets, knapsacks, and the contents of pant pockets were seized, and many of the items were pocketed by the searching guard. When they got to me, they took my knapsack, which held a few gifts I had purchased for Catherine in Manila and a bundle of her letters. They stole the trinkets and rifled through the letters, then threw them to the ground. I hated to see them care-lessly discarded because they were my only link to home. I couldn't do anything and was happy to have read and re-read them enough to almost have some things memorized. Surprisingly, I folded my fingers to hide my wedding band, and the guard missed seeing it. The looting continued down the line, and any resisting or pleading got answered by a punch, slap, or bamboo caning.

A few guards trooped up and down the line, pulling out the taller and bigger men to whom they gave terrible thrashings. Tom and I guessed the smaller Japs wanted to humiliate or torture the big fellows. The bamboo bearers continued to walk around and deliver indiscriminate whacks with their sticks. One took a swipe at me, but I ducked in time, and Tom took the hit right in his nose. As he wiped his bloody snoot, Tom punched me and commented, "Thanks a helluva lot, Charlie." During all the jostling, I kept expecting and hoping Jap trucks would roll in with food, but, boy oh boy, was I wrong. As Filipino, American, and Allied soldiers kept drifting in from the woods and company areas, I was surprised by their number. There seemed to be thousands upon thousands surrendering. While the cool morning air gave way to the tropical heat, we stood around for hours waiting. Tom wiped his bloody nose, grinned, and promised to return the favor someday. I was sweating heavily when an American officer came along and told us to quickly discard any Jap money or souvenirs because an English-speaking Jap officer had just told him the penalty for possession was immediate execution. We didn't have anything, but it wasn't long before we heard screaming followed by gunshots. After a few more anguished cries and shots, we realized his warning wasn't a bunch of bunk. Another American officer came along telling everyone to cooperate fully, look out for our buddies, and remain in single file once we were placed in formation.

Eventually the Jap guards got us lined up in a single-file formation, motioned, and used their rifle butts to shove us forward. Our walk began. It was a hot, cloudless day, and the road instantly became a dust bin as our steps soon kicked up the dry dirt. Enemy sentries marched along the line harassing the slower men and tormenting others with real or feigned punches and slaps. Spitting on prisoners was another nasty little insult, and it got worse when several enemy soldiers picked out a man and competed to see who could splatter the largest wad to his face. I witnessed a captain from our outfit who refused to hand over his shiny ring. The guard slammed him to the ground, and despite the effort of two sentries, the captain continued to resist; then out of no-where another guard produced a wire cutter, and they cut off his ring finger. The poor guy cried like hell as the guards laughed, and while one of them pocketed the bloodied ring, another shoved the severed finger deep into his mouth. The captain choked momentarily but ripped part of his shirt to bandage his finger and struggled to his feet. The way things were shaping up, whenever any prisoner got out of line or attempted to help another, the penalty would be a beating. There was nothing we could do to help the officer, but he knew it, and after getting back in line, he resumed his march-ing. In those first few hours, Tom and I saw some gruesome things. Men too slow to keep up with the pace were beaten, and if they failed to move any faster, they were shoved to the side of the road and bayoneted several times and died. Soldiers still in hospital smocks became easy targets for tor-ture and bayoneting. Despite pleading from nurses begging for mercy, they got none. As we slowly shuffled along, we glanced back in horror as one son-of-a-bitch guard after an-other bayoneted our slower or weaker buddies in the chest or back until their moaning stopped.

Since the beginning of this march we had gotten no food or water, and rest came only when the line temporarily slowed to a stop. On the afternoon of the first day, I experienced leg cramps and whispered to Tom my fear of failing to keep up. First he told me to shut up since talking in line was for-bidden, and then he wrapped his arm around my waist and kept me upright and moving until the cramping eased. As the hours dragged on, I noticed our original single-file formation had slowly turned into men marching two, three, or four abreast. Slow-moving Jap trucks carrying troops or supplies and jeep-like vehicles rumbled by and increased the choking dust. I was already using part of my shirt to protect my head from sunburn and began using it to shield my nose and mouth from sucking in too much swirling dust. As we moved along, Tom and I cautiously watched out for guards and whispered back and forth. Our best exchange was our mutual agreement to stick together no matter what the coming days might bring.

As the afternoon wore on, we heard more pitiful screams and an occasional gunshot, and witnessed many more acts of cruelty. It was just getting dark when the sentries motioned us to get off the road. Along with everyone else, I collapsed to the ground, relieved to get off my feet. Before I could fully catch my breath, I felt a boot to my ribs and stared up at a guard standing over me. He motioned me to stand, and as I did he grabbed my hand. Evidently, this guard had seen my wedding band earlier and had decided to make it his own. I knew not to resist, and he grunted as he yanked it off my finger. I flopped again into the dirt and felt this was the final insult of a terrible day. I knew the ring was only a symbol, but it hurt a lot to have this wedding gift from Catherine taken away. A little later I heard shouting, and Tom roused me to see what was happening. A slow-moving truck came along, and laughing Japs were slinging out shovelfuls of what looked like food. I ran and grabbed a big gob of the mush. It didn't smell so good and looked like rice with bits of fish or meat, but I ate it anyway and even found a clump on the ground that I also swallowed. My stomach reacted badly, and I resisted vomiting because this was my only nourishment since the day before. Then the truck sped up and disappeared. Though Tom and I ate some of the stuff, another man said he was sure it was simply their food garbage, and he wasn't going to eat their trash. He may have been right, but this crap was the only food-like thing we'd get during this entire march.

Lying on my back and trying to rest, I thought about my six months in the Philippines and how much things had changed. From getting bombed off Clark Field, retreating to Bataan, and then getting beaten to the point of surrender to being force-marched down a dusty road to God knows where, I had to acknowledge it had been a mighty tough six months. But I considered my earlier years as an orphan, a street hoodlum, and a CCC roustabout, and it seemed I had survived all those rough and tumble times, and I'd simply have to do my best to get past this terrible mess. I was also reminded of a recent little poem someone had written, which was circulating among the fellas:

> We're the battling bastards of Bataan
>
> We're the battling bastards of Bataan.
>
> No mama, no papa, no Uncle Sam.
>
> No aunts, no uncles, no cousins, no nieces,
>
> no pills, no planes, no artillery pieces,
>
> and nobody gives a damn.
>
> Nobody gives a damn.

Later I learned this limerick was penned by Frank Hewlett in 1942. He was the Manila bureau chief for United Press International and the last reporter to leave Corregidor before it fell to the Japanese. His wife was a POW, and he clearly understood our hopeless situation and frustration. I believe we did our best at Bataan, even though we didn't get much help from our Uncle Sam. Our prolonged resistance surely disrupted and delayed the enemies' war plans.

Sleep that first night of what became known as the Bataan Death March was difficult. I remember moments thinking and dreaming of my darling wife and all the good things back home. Then I experienced spasms of nightmarish images of the butchery and cruelty of our Japanese captors I had just witnessed.

Bataan Death March - POW Prison

On the morning of my second day as a POW and for days thereafter, a miserable routine of no food or water coupled with heat and unpredictable guards marked every step of our march. To wake us the Nips started shouting orders in Japanese, kicking and poling anyone slow to rise. This wake-up happened before sunrise. Then we were lined up four abreast in the middle of the road. After an hour or two, the column became three abreast and sometimes just a single file. The guards continually screamed "speedo," which meant to go quickly. Luckily, I found a few rags on the side of the road, and Tom and I used these to cover our heads from the blazing sun. Many men suffered severe sunburn and blistering. Once a blister or sore burst open blood and puss oozed out and flies swarmed the wound. In the tropics without medicine, untreated wounds easily became infected by filthy bugs and dirt. I believe many men died from these infections. Several times during the march I felt ready to collapse because my legs would cramp and feel like two hundred-pound logs. After struggling through the pain for a while, the feeling of excessive weight and twisted muscles would slowly diminish. This happened to me every day as we marched away from Bataan.

As the guards pushed and prodded their captives, they occasionally singled out a man for beating. There was no pattern or reason for the random violence, and the threat hung like a dark cloud and made me extremely nervous. Sometimes it was a rifle butt thrust to the gut or a bamboo thrashing to the head or legs. These cruel attacks could involve a single hit or many blows by one guard or several. Tom and I got whacked a few times for no apparent reason but just kept moving forward, trying our best to maintain our composure by not fighting back or even eyeing our attacker. Many men who stumbled along couldn't or wouldn't get up and were either beaten or bayoneted to death. The only time I remember Japs firing their guns was when someone attempted to run away. After a while it seemed some of the men knew damn well it was suicide to try to escape, but they tried anyway. I understood their desperation but never their reasons, and I would never judge any of them. Nobody was certain what direction we were heading, but it seemed we were moving north. Dust continued to be a daily torment as cavalry pieces and trucks rumbled past us. A few quick downpours allowed us a break from our thirst, but any rain was quickly followed by more heat and humidity. Along the road Jap soldiers were busy setting up antiaircraft guns and big 105s. I think the guns were pointed directly at Corregidor, which was south of Mariveles. General MacArthur's headquarters fortress was evidently still resisting the Japs. Tom suggested we might be a human shield to protect the columns of enemy troops marching with us from Corregidor's artillery. A day or two later, we began to hear the big Jap guns blasting away at the Rock and incoming explosions from the guns on Corregidor.

Guards were spaced every fifty feet or so along our column. A few spoke some English and tried to get conversations going with their captives. Other guards verbally taunted prisoners in words nobody understood. Tom and I quickly learned to keep moving and avoid eye contact with any of our captors. It seemed some of the guards looked for any excuse to assault a prisoner, especially the Filipinos. As we passed through barrios, villagers lined the roads and silently watched as we marched down the road. Many of the people looked sad, and I saw more little children and women than men and boys. A few women offered cups of water and bits of food as we passed by, but they were slapped away by the guards. When a Filipino was able to successfully pass something to a prisoner, they were both pulled aside and beaten. The local people were defenseless, and it was apparent from their facial expressions and gestures that they intensely hated the Japanese. So the march continued hour after hour with few stops.

We had to pee while walking, hoping a guard wouldn't notice and we wouldn't pee on any fellows nearby. Although most of us had empty stomachs, we crapped at night and used leaves and pieces of paper to clean ourselves. The poor guys suffering with diarrhea or dysentery lacked bowel control and soiled their clothes. Flies followed their stench, and the men became covered with flies. The number of dead men in the ditches increased with each passing mile. I'll never forget seeing several small Filipino boys lying on their backs just off the trail. They had evidently been beaten and bayo- neted numerous times, but the grimace on their little faces revealed they had endured torture. I saw men gurgling blood who had been thrown to the ditches and were dying. Groups of killed men were visible from time to time in neat lines just off the road, displaying numerous bayonet wounds in their backs. Later we learned a detail of guards at the end of our line killed any stragglers or wounded prisoners. We called these bastards the "buzzard patrol." It was tough seeing such cruelty and being in a helpless situation where even helping a fallen buddy could result in getting stomped. I decided that surviving was the only thing I could do to defy my cruel captors. However, as the miles continued and the number of fatalities piled up, I began to wonder if this march was designed to kill all the prisoners in a torturous march to no- where. I spent hours daydreaming about Catherine and her mother's pork chops, fried chicken, and potato salad to avoid the awful sights and smells. I honestly believe through all the heat, stink, depression, and thirst, with the Lord's help, visions of better times kept me upright and my feet moving forward step after step.

One day we passed an artesian well only a few yards off the trail, and several men bolted and were immediately shot in the back. They knew without hearing the command "fus a goo" which meant stop, they were taking a serious chance. But thirst was so intense that some men did crazy things, went all to pieces, and ran for the water. Tom and I were told by an Aussie to find a few pebbles and roll them around in our mouths to decrease our insatiable thirst. We did, and it actu- ally helped a little. One afternoon, nearing a small creek, we were stopped and herded toward water. Along with everyone else, I rushed to the stream. I sucked up the water despite its pinkish color. Looking around, I noticed bloated bodies lying along the banks and in the water. Swarms of vultures were tearing chunks of flesh that bloodied the stream. It was a sickening, horrible sight. But I think we all realized that getting hydrated, even in a bloody creek, was necessary to survive the heat and physical exertion of the forced march. Everyone sucked in the foul water until the guards pushed us back in line.

The roads at times were narrow, and we heard "fus a goo" many times as large Jap vehicles and cavalry pieces rumbled along the trail. The mountains and hills of Bataan reminded me of those in Virginia and West Virginia where I worked in a CCC camp. Unlike home, however, large parts of these hills had been torn to pieces by constant shelling. Many sick fellows struggled to keep moving. Several were helped by other men. Tom and I got to propping up one young man from Washington DC. He was weak from malaria and had a heavily bandaged leg that was oozing red. At times we dragged him along, and in whispers he told us about his family and sweetheart. He was a nice kid, and I sure wish I could remember his name. Anyway, we helped him along for a good while, trying to hide him from any guard's notice. However, after a few hours, a Jap guard suddenly got in our face and shouted, "Speedo, speedo." He shoved Tom and I aside and screamed at the fellow we were helping. The kid tried several times to rise but eventually crumpled to the ground. We knew he was weak and in bad shape but hoped we could somehow keep him going. Tom and I tried to get him to his feet despite the guard's interference, but we were repeatedly shoved away. We begged him to stand up, and then we heard him say meekly, "Thanks." I knew what was coming next and looked away as the guard repeatedly bayoneted him. We heard his final weak outcry and moan. It was terrible, but there was nothing more Tom and I could do. This situation left me feeling awful as Tom and I were pushed back in line. Terrible things like this happened a lot. I am ashamed to say that after a few days of witnessing so much savagery, I got numb from seeing so much cruelty and death. I accepted the fact that I was powerless to help or save those who couldn't keep up or decided to run. This truly became a survival-of-the-fittest situation.

Except for the first night, we never received anything to eat from our captors during the entire death march. Passing through little hamlets, some Filipinos continued to offer leaves filled with rice. However, experience had quickly taught us the painful or deadly consequences if we dared to accept anything. The guards seemed almost eager to inflict punishment on villagers offering food or soldiers accepting their small gifts. The sentries did everything they could to prevent us from getting anything and pushed the natives away from our column. Whenever we got close to what had recently been a front line, there were more bodies. Many had begun to decompose. The dead had skin blackened by the sun and faces eaten away by maggots and birds. It was hard to tell if the corpses were Filipinos, Japs, or Americans. Some men were lying facedown, some lying faceup. Some of dead were slouched over in blown-up trucks and jeeps. Gnats, blowflies, and squawking crows were all over these scenes of death. I vividly recall seeing one man hanging from a telephone pole. His fatigue shirt bore army corporal stripes. His skin was blackened and had begun to fall away from his body. His scalp had fallen halfway down his face, and a sea of squirming maggots squirmed all over his body. I saw many awful things. These sights and smells of death sadly became too familiar along our march. I began to reconcile the horror by realizing I was simply seeing empty shells of flesh with their spirits and souls now residing in a better place faraway. Occasionally someone in line would attempt to retrieve a dead soldier's dog tags, but punishment followed if a guard witnessed this action. We were taught in basic training to take a deceased comrade's dog tags so the individual's family could be informed. It was the right thing to do, but even this simple military procedure was denied by our captors. Combat had proven so fierce along some stretches of the trail that I observed squashed and flattened bodies and body parts littering the roadway. As we stepped along, we had to avoid stepping into the putrid bodies. The stench of death became so bad in places, it burned my nostrils and watered my eyes. I didn't want anything dead to touch or smear my shoes or pants, so we all carefully moved around the gruesome carnage. At times I wondered if what I was seeing and experiencing might be the closest thing to hell. Unfortunately, in the coming months, I would see and experience worse things.

As best I can remember, it was the fourth or fifth day of the march when I truly thought I had walked my last steps. I was exhausted, sore, dizzy, and shaky. But my faithful buddy kept me standing and slowly moving forward. Thank God Tom was there to help and talk me through my weakest moments. As the Japs ran around hollering and bashing heads, Tom told me to think of Jesus Christ and his walk to Calvary. He told me God's son was beaten, humiliated, and spat upon, but he bravely trudged forward. He said we should do our utmost to follow his example. The encouragement he offered motivated me to endure the next few dreadful days. Tom usually didn't talk much religion, but several times his words gave me comfort and hope. As I slowly trekked along, accompanied by thirst and an empty belly, I concentrated on Jesus carrying his cross and the suffering he endured for me. I began to think surviving my ordeal would give an important signal to my Japanese tormentors that I would resist their inhumane treatment and survive to fight another day. Of course I wanted to live, but more importantly I didn't want these cruel soldiers to beat me or ever step foot in America. I made my inspiration the example of a suffering Jesus, and my intention, with his help, was to survive and do whatever I could to stop these bastards. Daydreaming about Catherine, home, Mrs. Williams's wonderful cooking, and my brothers also comforted me enough to endure the daily suffering. In this lousy predicament, I guess it was natural to look inward and beg for God's help. Since I had little control over what the Japs might do, I resigned myself to do my best and simply trust the Lord.

Once we got beyond the front battlefront areas, there were fewer bodies and less stomach-wrenching scenes and stink. One night, as a gang of us huddled in the grass, whispering began. No one dared talk too loud, as this was another possible offense that could result in punishment, so we whispered. One regular army Filipino soldier stated his belief in a massive prisoner exchange that would set us free. Another fellow spoke with confidence about MacArthur finally getting a huge fleet and reinforcements sent to our rescue. An American civilian complained it was a damn shame President

Roosevelt had evidently abandoned the Philippines and didn't send us help. Somebody else believed a large prison was our ultimate destination. Of course, all the mumbling opinions and speculations were guesses. Talk also turned to Betty Grable's measurements, the World Series, all the delicious past Christmas dinners, and other pleasant topics about home, wives, girlfriends, and children. At night in quiet voices, these conversations, though often a litany of rumors and good memories of home, provided daily relief from the daytime miseries. I did enjoy concentrating on my Kakie Baby, our future life together, and friends back home. Such thoughts proved to relieve some of the nervousness that had become an unwelcome condition.

Some guards, especially the smaller ones, continued to pick on the larger men among their columns of prisoners. Certain Jap sentries seemed to find pleasure in taunting and humiliating the bigger captives. In addition to beatings and getting spat on, I witnessed a guard forcing a big fellow to pull down his pants and expose his private parts. Laughing, the guard then smashed the poor man in his groin several times with his clenched fist. When the prisoner collapsed to the ground, several other guards rushed to the scene and stood over the half-naked, injured man and laughed like hyenas. At such moments we could only seethe inside, as any visible reactions of disgust or anger would simply result in getting physical abuse. When I was a kid, I envied my taller brothers, but at this time I was thankful to be a small man. I began to wonder, based upon their outrageous behavior, about the military status of some of these guards. Not surprising, it was revealed later that many guards assigned to this detail were flunkies and misfits found unfit for the regular infantry.

In our section of the marching troops, we had a few weirdo Japs. One mumbled incessantly, and another carried a fixed, almost frozen, goofy smile on his face. Often the sentries argued violently and wrestled among themselves, and their superiors routinely knocked them to the ground and forced them to rigidly stand at attention. Many of the guards were as dirty and sloppy as the prisoners.

On a few days, the march was stopped when an obstacle in the road had to be moved or when a Japanese commander decided to allow his guards a rest. To stave off our hunger, Tom and I began to eat grass and pick at small crawling bugs and beetles. Some of the stuff tasted all right, but other things caused us to gag. We began to learn the plants and bugs our stomachs would accept. It was crazy but necessary to have some nourishment and energy. On one insufferable hot day, sprawled in a field bordered by tall bamboo, I looked around and realized a bunch of us looked like grazing goats. It seems kind of funny now, remembering grown men munching on plants and bugs, but by God it was really a miserable situation. I had no idea how much, but along with others I was losing weight. My ribs were sticking out, and the growling in my stomach became a steady chorus of weird sounds. While starving saps the body's strength, I also felt it effected clear thinking because there were days, as I stumbled along, that I seemed to wake up feeling my mind had quit my body and I was a robot. With daily temperatures well into the nineties, coupled with suffocating humidity, I lost track of time and the number of days we had been marching. However, Tom seemed to know the number of days we had marched, our general direction, and the day's hour. He told me he had been a Boy Scout and had a good feel for such things. He figured the time and distance we covered by calculating our approximate walking speed and the hours we marched between sunrise and sundown. We joked and argued about his calculations, but he was confident in his numbers. Brief downpours provided only a few minutes of cooling relief and valuable drops of moisture, but they also stirred up mosquitoes and flies. It was April and the dry season, so rain showers were infrequent and never lasted long.

Somehow and somewhere along our journey, Tom and I reunited with our 803rd buddies, Steve and Red. It was good to see these guys and know they had survived our deadly walk. They knew nothing about where we were heading or when our retreat from Bataan might end. Steve did relate part of a conversation he heard between an English-speaking Japanese officer and an American major that indicated we were heading for a camp. Like everyone else, Steve had to move forward, and he couldn't share more of his overheard discussion until our evening stop. As the atrocities and grueling parade continued, I was silently praying while rolling the tiny rocks around in my mouth when a guard shoved me from behind, and I swallowed my stones. Tom thought it was hilarious and joked he had heard of kidney stones but never stomach stones.

Soon I saw men openly weeping, and I honestly believe a few went mad from the physical and mental strain of our ordeal. One example I observed was a nearby soldier who was steady on his feet but staring straight ahead as if in a trance. We talked that evening, and I was surprised he had only been married a few weeks, as Catherine and I had been, before getting shipped overseas. His name was Robert, and he was from South Carolina and seemed a pretty normal person. However, the very next day I saw him striding along again as if hypnotized, and without saying a damn thing, he casually stepped away from the column. Within a few seconds, he walked up to a guard and punched him right smack in the nose. The guard, bloodied and on his rear end, quickly jumped up and swung his bayonet, which slashed Robert's throat. The blow caused a violent gush of blood from his jugular vein, and he probably was dead shortly after hitting the ground. It was frightening to witness because he seemed completely normal the night before. I'm not sure, but perhaps his hypnotic stare indicated something bad going on his mind. Sadly, there were other men like Robert. Things like this tragic incident left me convinced that some prisoners in our number had become so frustrated and depressed, they chose a moment to strike out, knowing the fatal consequences. Some among us surely lost hope, and while their bodies could've survived, their spirits collapsed.

We continued the trek that seemed endless. As we passed through little villages, more Filipinos appeared and attempted to give us food. On many occasions I saw sentries grab the food and eat it or slam it to the ground. If we were lucky, we'd snatch a morsel when a guard wasn't looking. I knew to swallow quickly and not be seen by a guard. The locals also tried to give us water, but when the guards intervened, a few villagers hurled water our way, and the drops were a small blessing. It was routine for guards to roughly handle any kind people trying to help us. We were told later by someone who had seen it firsthand that Filipinos were actually beaten to death by guards when they tried to help prisoners. The courage and acts of generosity offered by these natives reinforced my feelings they were generally good and loving people. We continued to pass roadside wells every few miles and near barrios. Some had buckets, and a few were rigged with spigots. I still consider it inhumane that the Japanese did not allow us a few minutes of clean water at these watering holes. The guards would flock to the wells to fill their canteens and splash their faces and heads, but we were never allowed. In addition to this cruelty, every time we got within sight of a well, a few of our number would break out of line and race to the water. In every instance, I witnessed these men getting shot in the back. One evening, a college boy who had lived in Japan prior to the war told us a few interesting things that reinforced our understanding of the Japanese military. According to him, their soldier code forbade surrendering and required suicide before giving in to an enemy. Also their rules of warfare stipulated that prisoners were to be treated as cowards and given no mercy. He wasn't sure but thought the Japanese government had never agreed to any treaties or rules governing the humane treatment of war prisoners.

By the sixth day, according to Tom's count, things were looking mighty glum. I was increasingly nervous and jittery, and other fellows in our group seemed equally agitated. The destination of this long march remained a mystery to everyone except the Japanese commanders running things. Hunger, parched throats, and despair became our constant companions. Hour after hour and day after day we ate dust while seeing rotted bodies along the roadside. Buzzards and crows floated overhead ready for easy pickings from the corpses and perhaps us. By this point in our march, we weren't talking much and simply walked until ordered to stop. Then we flopped into the dirt and became motionless heaps until the guards yelled and beat us to resume our trek the next morning. In addition to our ragged and soiled clothes, our shoes and boots were now coming apart, and our stink was drawing lots of bugs. The soles of my shoes were flopping as the stitching unraveled. Sucking our pebbles and hearing "speedo" a hundred times a day, we stumbled along. Then, late one morning, we walked into the little town of San Fernando.

We shuffled through the town until we reached a rail yard. The tracks were jammed with boxcars and small locomotives. The sentries directed us to the boxcars, and I thought we might at last stop and have a chance to get off our feet. As our long line stopped and bunched up into groups, guards began to separate us into smaller groups. Tom and I stuck together, but in all the confusion, I lost sight of Steve and Red. With jabs and punches, we were shoved into the metal boxcars. We were crammed in like cows or pigs heading for slaughter. We were so tightly packed, there was no room to stoop or sit. Standing was our only choice, and it was so crowded that each man's body supported other men. The sick and weak were held erect only because we were jammed in so tightly. After the last were pushed into the boxcar, the door was pulled shut. Our space became dark except for thin shafts of light glaring through cracks in the wooden walls. There was little air flow, so our body odors quickly filled the space. Then we waited an hour or two before moving as the other boxcars were filled. With a jolt our car finally jerked into motion, and our journey began. The train moved painfully slow, and the cars and tracks creaked and groaned with every turn and lurch. We still had no idea where we were going.

After an hour or two, the level of noxious air increased since many peed, crapped, or vomited while standing in the incredibly confined space. While I prayed under my breath, many others were also mumbling prayers. Cries and groans signaled men were suffering or dying on their feet. A few men grumbled, cursed, and pushed for more space, but there was no extra room. Men standing next to the metal exterior of the boxcar suffered extra because the sun baked the metal. I realized it was hopeless to waste my energy complaining or fighting this miserable situation, so I patiently stood in my small space. A few men standing near the sliding doors tried unsuccessfully to move them open, but the doors were locked and wouldn't budge. After four or five hours, the train finally slowed and squealed to a stop. When the door slid open, the sudden sensation of fresh air was refreshing; however, the sudden sunlight was blinding. Men quickly jumped off the train, some pushed, and a few tumbled out onto the ground. Glancing back inside, I saw three or four men heaped on the floor. I think they may have died and collapsed when the overcrowded car emptied. It seemed a hell of a shame that after suffering a march of seven or eight days, covering over sixty-five miles, some of our buddies would die in a damned boxcar. If the Japs had used open rail cars or ones with ventilation, more would have survived. Though many Americans and Filipinos survived the long march, many perished along its route.

We arrived at Camp O'Donnell in the middle of April 1942. After almost two weeks without decent food or water, many of us were sick and walking skeletons. Protruding rib bones and pencil-thin legs and arms, in addition to sunken faces, sum up our general appearance. Filipino prisoners were sent to a separate prison camp nearby. An American officer told us the camp had once been a US Army training base, but it was converted into a huge prison by the Japanese when they overran the place. Towering barbed wire fences circled the camp, and Nip guards with machine guns and rifles patrolled the perimeter or were stationed in little elevated shacks along the fences. The camp area was composed of grassy fields, patches of bare earth, and low muddy places. This POW camp was close to Tarlac. By the time Tom and I got there, the place was already crowded. Housing consisted of old wooden barracks, lean-to huts, and tents supported by bamboo poles. There was no netting to fend off the mosquitoes, and the roofs leaked every time it rained. We were still wearing the same clothes worn the day of our surrender, and our shirts and pants were ragged and literally coming apart. Supplied bed coverings were riddled with filth, fleas, and bedbugs. Some nights I slept on the floor or ground to avoid the constant gnawing of insects. Some officers stayed together while others freely mixed in with the regular soldiers. Nobody wore their stripes or bars at this point, so there was no saluting. A handful of our senior officers did get recognition from the Jap commanders, but they had little influence on how things were run. We had no showers, and our only chance to bathe was to strip naked during a rainstorm and use our hands to scrub off the filth. The only fresh water came from a few spigots. All day and night men lined up for water, but the Jap guards only allowed us a cupful at a time. The water pressure in the tiny pipes was low and produced only a slow trickle, but everyone waited patiently for their cupful. On our second or third day, while lined up for water, Tom and I caught up with Steve and Red, and it was mighty good to see they had survived the terrible hike and train ride from San Fernando.

During the middle of the day, the camp became extremely humid, and this added to our misery because it drew out thousands of stinging mosquitoes and flies. The camp was absolutely filthy. Simple open ditches served as our toilets, and during afternoon downpours, the human waste would overflow the trenches and flood parts of the camp. The sanitation problem was compounded by the fact that many of the sickest men lost control of their bowels and bladders. They simply had no control, which meant you had to constantly watch your step walking along the pathways. We got one daily meal, and that was a small portion of mushed rice with small flecks of vegetables and unknown meat. The food never smelled good, but I ate every bit, realizing every morsel kept me from starving and provided some nutrition. Some guys foolishly traded their food portion for a cigarette butt or a taste of homemade hooch. We lived in so much hunger, and none of the gruel ever went to waste. There also wasn't much medicine or doctoring at Camp O'Donnell. A handful of our doctors and medics did their best, but they had practically no supplies. Tom and I heard whatever medical supplies the Japs had were used only for their officers, and the tiny amount passed through the fences went to our officers or the highest bidder. There was a pitiful building called the Z ward, and this held the terminally ill, badly injured, and diseased men in quarantine until they died. Nobody survived the zero ward. It was an awful place but perhaps necessary to prevent healthy men from contracting diseases and germs. Every day litters bearing the dead exited the ward while more barely alive men arrived. I heard up to a hundred men died there some days. The only doctoring inside the ward came from medics and a few doctors doing their best to clean wounds and perform some simple medical procedures. However, they didn't have any medicine, had few medical tools, and worked in a filthy tent.

Every morning we lined up and were counted. This was to ensure no absences from overnight escapes or hiding. Upon arriving at Camp O'Donnell, we were told the camp rules by an English-speaking Jap. He stressed the most important rule was to not attempt running away. He shouted that anyone caught trying to escape would be immediately executed, and anyone who escaped would be executed once captured. We were forced to watch as a few men were tortured, beheaded, or shot because they attempted to get away or briefly escaped. I think our enemy felt that forcing us to watch the punishment ensured compliance with their rules. Although we were weak and unarmed, I can tell you for sure that there wasn't a night when we didn't talk about escaping. Tom favored working out a good way to bug out. He endlessly discussed where a section of fence could be breached or burrowed under. He watched and timed the marching sentries patrolling the perimeter fences. I felt our chances were lousy and resisted seriously considering any of his schemes. After some morning formations, a Nip officer would closely inspect us and pull out a number of men. They were quickly hustled to waiting trucks, which sped away through the camp gates, or were sent off for special jobs. We guessed, but nobody knew, what this was all about, but the men who left by trucks were never seen again. On my second or third day of imprisonment, Tom and I got pulled out of the morning formation. We didn't board a truck but got assigned to the burial detail.

When a man died, the first thing that occurred was someone collected his dog tags and passed them along to an officer. Unfortunately, many men had lost their tags or had them taken as souvenirs by the Japs during our march. In this case the dead man's buddies or anyone who knew him would give whatever information they had to an officer. Once the dead man had been identified, any usable clothing or shoes would be removed from his body and distributed to anyone needing same. My job was to help haul the dead a few hundred yards from the main part of the camp for burial in a swampy area. I also helped dig the ditches in which to lay their bodies. We used ditches rather than individual graves because there were just too many dead. The trenches we dug began to ooze water because the water table was high, so the dead were laid to rest in puddles of mud. It was hard and disheartening work. We always paused for a few quiet seconds after depositing each body, despite guards insisting we hurry. Occasionally, if a chaplain or someone who knew the deceased was present, a few words were spoken. With so many bodies to bury, it was always a rush job to just keep up, and it was exhausting work. When monsoon rains came, we spent part of the next day reburying bodies that floated out of the ground. This was a big problem and nasty work. We placed rocks and chunks of concrete on the graves to hold the bodies down in the soggy earth, but this didn't guarantee that they wouldn't pop out of the ground. Also, wild dogs and other beasts tore at the flesh of the floating corpses at night, and these mangled bodies had to be reburied. We tried to dig the graves a little deeper, but the burial area was a hopeless field of mud. Our pitiful shovels just couldn't penetrate and hold back the muck from sliding back into the ditches. The only way I got through this gruesome job was to continually think that the souls of these poor men had gone faraway to a good place of happiness and no more misery.

As the days passed, I was getting skinnier and weaker. Even with a little water and food every day, I thought my health was drifting away. One morning I woke up and could hardly get to my feet. My head was pounding, and I experienced spasms of chills and hot flashes. My eyes and nose were oozing fluid, and I'm sure I had a fever. Thankfully, Tom got me to the morning formation, and I was able to spend the rest of that day lying around, but I remained drowsy and sick a few more days. From what I learned talking to others and a medic, my sudden sickness may have been malaria. A few days later I felt much better, but I was worried since I didn't know much about malaria except it could be deadly. A few days later Steve also had a bout of what everyone said was malaria.

Some of our highest-ranking officers and chaplains were allowed to meet with the camp commander and begged for more water, food, medicine, cigarettes, better shelter, and a more decent way to handle our sick and bury our dead comrades. From what I observed, things didn't get any better the whole time I was at Camp O'Donnell. Every morning the Japs lined us up, and we heard "Ichi, ni, san, shi, go, roku, shichi, hachu, ku, ju." This was Japanese for one to ten, and it was how they checked our numbers to ensure no one was missing. Then several officers would march in a high-step fashion to the front of the formation, and the bowing and shouting between enlisted and officer Japs would begin. Back and forth it would go. First the enlisted men in charge would bow to the officers, then the officers would bow, and then orders would be shouted. While I knew the little bastards were cruel, their displays of shouting and bowing were funny as hell. A few times, if an enlisted guard didn't respond correctly or bow deeply enough, an officer would get in his face and slap the crap out of him or knock the poor sucker to the ground. While I found their behavior odd and funny, nobody dared laugh or show any amusement.

One afternoon, near the fence that enclosed the camp, Tom and I watched small Japanese aircraft practice landings and takeoffs. The single-engine planes would rumble down the grass field, make a few loops, and then hop and skip to a landing. We got to laughing as a two-man plane made an especially rough landing, bounced all over the place, and damn near flipped over. As the men exited the plane, an officer ran up and commenced screaming holy hell. The men began to furiously bow, and out of the blue this superior began to slap the snot out of each one, but they kept on bowing. Tom and I began to laugh like hell at this spectacle of Japanese military behavior. It really felt good and was probably the first time we had laughed in a long time. Unbeknownst to us, a Jap officer witnessed our fun, and we quickly hushed as he approached. We feared big trouble was coming our way. Well, this guy wasn't smiling as he gripped the handle of his sheathed sword, and I worried something terrible was about to happen. But, to our surprise and relief, this officer chuckled and in excellent English told us we would not be laughing if we knew the latest news. He announced that the Imperial Japanese Army had just invaded California and sunk more of our navy ships. He told us that the war was going badly for America, and if we ever got home, we might have to learn the Japanese language and customs. Obviously, we were stunned by his comments. Having our full attention, he told us he was a UCLA graduate and knew a lot about our country. He then bragged that when Washington DC was captured, we wouldn't be so happy. I listened, not knowing how to respond to this awful news or load of bullshit he was throwing our way. The officer pulled out and lit a cigarette. He talked a lot about his experiences in America, and I finally felt comfortable enough to make a comment. I told him, "Sir, when you bomb Washington, please tell them we are here and still waiting for their help." Then this damn Jap officer laughed and laughed and finally walked away. At the time, I was dead serious about my comment. I was bitter that so many good men had been abandoned and were suffering, waiting for MacArthur and Roosevelt to send help. When I heard the little poem, "The Battling Bastards of Bataan," I felt it was true we were bastards without our parents, America, helping us during our defense of the Bataan Peninsula.

Over the next few days, we witnessed increased cruelty from the guards. Some of the bastards loved to taunt and torture. Once day I saw guards gather up three tall prisoners and march them to a barbed wire fence, where they were ordered to line up. Next the guards stepped back a few paces, shouted orders, raised their rifles, slowly took aim, and pulled the triggers of their rifles. Nothing happened because their guns were unloaded. However, the horrified and mournful faces of our boys thinking they were about to die was a terrible sight. On another occasion, we saw some of our men being used for bayonet practice. The guards made up a contest in which each would make a bayonet thrust to see who could get the closest to touching the chest of the prisoner. Our men were tied to poles and didn't know what was going to happen. In this cruel game, some men were wounded, and we heard a few actually died while the guards laughed.

Looking back, I think Camp O'Donnell was the closest thing to hell I ever experienced. Hunger, thirst, torture, and sickness hung over the place like a cloud. Many good men suffered, lost hope, and died in that damned place. When you heard a gunshot or a scream, you knew someone had tried to escape and was being tortured or executed. With few exceptions the guards and officers in this hellhole were nasty sons of bitches. Tom and I concluded that many of the sentries were dumbbells unfit for regular army service. We gave some of them nicknames, which we thought defined their appearance or behavior. I remember the names Big Ears, Monkey Face, Ugly Duck, and Mickey Mouse. Naturally we had to be absolutely sure they knew no English; then we could politely bow and nicely address them by their pet name or, with a smile, tell them to go to hell or eat shit. It was a humorous game until the Jap guards got schooled on our curse words. After a few beatings, we stopped this practice. One evening Tom, who had a good singing voice, was singing a little song for our enjoyment, and a guard came along. The guard ordered Tom to sing him a song, saying, "You sing for me; you sing for me." Well, without hesitation, Tom began a vigorous rendition of "The Star-Spangled Banner." The guard listened for a few seconds and then slapped the hell out of Tom, shouting, "You no sing 'Star-Spangled Banner,'" before storming away.

During the day, along the fence, curious children hung around watching activities in the prison, and Filipino women often tried to pass bits of food, medicine, or handwritten notes. It was risky because when a sentry observed such activity, he quickly rushed in and jabbed the butt of his rifle often injuring an innocent civilian simply trying to help. Often at night we invariably talked about our wives, girlfriends, family, and good American food. I believe the conversations kept our hopes and spirits alive, as we lived in a hellish reality. A few men wrote letters home even though we had no means to send or receive letters from our loved ones. Usually the subject of escape became another big topic of discussion in the evening. None of us knew the overall war situation or what was going on outside our jail, but we realized life here would not end well based upon the terrible conditions. Some argued that escape was our only choice if we wished to survive. A few talked about tunneling underneath the fences or rushing the gates when opened for incoming vehicles. Having seen and witnessed the punishment dealt to those who attempted escape did not deter the passionate arguments to get the hell away. Others felt we had no options and should hang on until we got liberated or the enemy improved our living conditions. I wasn't sure but knew full well if we broke away, the villages were likely occupied by Japs, and there were probably spies among the locals. Tom, Steve, and Red were strongly convinced escape was our only choice, and it was just a matter of finding the best plan and time to break away. Nothing was ever decided, but the talk of escape plans kept us thinking and helped us sleep a little better.

It was in my second week as a prisoner when a Nip officer slowly walked along our morning formation and randomly pulled men out of line. He counted in English, one, two, three, and I was number twenty-six and pulled from the ranks. He carefully eyed each of us with a head-to-toe inspection. Luckily, my 803rd buddies were also selected, and along with a few dozen other men, we were sent to an area away from the main formation. There this same officer ordered us to sit down. He then told us we had been chosen for an important job to help the army, his army. He added that this assignment would get us out of the camp, and if we performed well, we might get more food. He talked further about more privileges and other things, but the only thing getting my attention was the promise of more food. Observing the crew he had chosen, I believe we were picked because we appeared a little more fit than others. However, I thought we were still a miserable bunch of skinny men. At any rate, we had no option but to follow his orders.

After his little speech, several half-ton trucks rolled in, and we were shoved and motioned to climb aboard. I remember Red nervously joked that we had gotten a three-day pass to Manila; another guy asked a guard our destination and got a grunt in response. The trucks moved, and the camp gates opened wide as we rumbled onto a dusty road. The truck whined through its gears and puked a thick cloud of diesel fumes as our mysterious trip began. We were followed by a jeep loaded with three fully armed Jap soldiers. Our convoy rumbled along, and nobody had a clue about our new assignment or destination. Despite the uncertainties, I was relieved to leave Camp O'Donnell, and my buddies agreed. The fellows on board speculated what was going to happen next. I had seen other groups of men hauled away and never saw them return, and this was a troubling thought. Someone suggested they were pulling out those they considered the healthiest-looking men for execution, since they feared a revolt within the camp led by the strongest inmates. Others mentioned we were being exchanged for Japanese POWs. I thought both these possibilities unlikely since killing us could be easily done at the camp without the need for a truck ride. I couldn't imagine the Japs interested in trading prisoners since they were obviously in full control of the Islands. Other rumors and theories were kicked around, but I honestly felt we were headed for some kind of work detail.

After about an hour of bumping along in swirling dust, we finally slid to a stop. Guards then directed us to enter a large warehouse. Inside the building there were numerous boxes and bags, a pile of old clothes and boots, and a squad of pretty sharp-looking Nip soldiers. When the officer from the morning assembly marched in, the soldiers smartly shouldered their arms and snapped to attention. After their usual routine of bowing and grunting, the soldiers assumed a parade-rest formation, and the officer ordered us to sit. He then told us our assignment was to move supplies to locations in the nearby hills and mountains too remote for their trucks or where bridges and roads had been destroyed.

ROUTE OF BATAAN DEATH MARCH

Route of Bataan Death March

Slave Labor - Escape

It soon became apparent that we would be pack mules hauling boxes and bags of supplies to their remote garrisons and camps. In addition, the officer repeated the promise about getting more food if we performed well, but in the same breath he promised those who attempted escape would be executed on the spot. He also said our efforts would help the Empire of Japan serve its Filipino brothers and sisters. I thought this was a load of crap because my eyes had seen innumerable examples of Japs hating the Filipinos and the fear, anger, and resentment the Filipinos felt toward the Japanese. After thirty minutes of more threats and promises, the officer shut up, and his soldiers motioned us to a pile of clothes. I knew these items were stripped from dead Filipinos and Allied soldiers. From the smell and appearance, the clothes had evidently been sprayed with bleach or some kind of cleansing agent. As a group we all hesitated, I think, realizing the source of these items. But after a few minutes, we rummaged through the clothes and shoes. I found replacement shoes, a decent long-sleeve fatigue shirt, and a pair of trousers. Along with the others, I ripped off my soiled and torn clothes and put on the items from the heap of clothes. I understood the need for better garments and shoes despite the source. Next the Jap soldiers began rigging us to carry things. The hefty wooden boxes of ammo required a man to lie face down while guards wrapped ropes and straps across his chest and shoulders. Then the man would be pulled to his feet by two guards. The crates of ammo were the heaviest item, and the larger men were chosen for this load. Tom and Steve got ammo while Red and I were loaded with huge bags of rice that were soft but heavy. I had to stoop to my knees while the rice was plopped on and tied to my back. Some of the men fitted with ammo boxes simply couldn't stay on their feet, so they were unstrapped and fitted with smaller boxes or bags. Several men were unable to stand or maintain their balance with any load. These unfortunate guys were marched out the door by guards. Ten or fifteen minutes later we heard shots, and I suspected their fate.

One man whispered that we were being used as pack animals, and he was 100 percent correct. When everyone was squared away with their cargo, the guards marched us outdoors, and we began to hike along a narrow trail. Tom, Steve, Red, and I managed to remain together in the double-file line that later became a single file as the trail narrowed and we got tired. I guess my load was about fifty pounds, and Tom's crate of ammo maybe seventy pounds. In addition to the sentries, several donkeys pulled small carts of supplies and a guard or two, but most of the guards walked alongside and among the prisoners. Once we started walking, Steve mentioned we were near Tagudin, a little coastal town in a northern province. It was hilly, and green mountains topped by fog slowly became visible in the distance. He added this could be a good location because of stories floating around about Filipino and American guerrillas operating in the mountains. I had heard similar stories about men who had escaped from Bataan before our surrender and the death march. They high-tailed it off to the remote mountains to evade the enemy. According to these rumors, these men planned to eventually harass the small enemy garrisons and patrols nearby. There was no way to know if any of this was true, but it was nice to think friendly guerrillas might come to our rescue.

While it was good to be away from the filth and disease at Camp O'Donnell, it wasn't long before the heat and heavy load made me wonder if this new assignment was a better deal than sitting around the POW camp. We all knew the Japs wouldn't hesitate to waste anyone who tried to escape or became incapable of handling their load. It wasn't too many miles before the metal edges of the ammo box tore through Tom's shirt and ripped his skin. We had no padding or medicine, and because of the incessant flies and mosquitoes, I knew Tom's wounds could get infected. When our march rested, I traded loads with Tom to save his back from further gouging and was lucky the wooden crate didn't tear into my back. Every three or four hours our sweaty climb was halted to allow the donkeys and human pack animals a rest. The breaks were long enough for us to receive a cup of water and valuable moments to lie down. In my opinion, stopping a few times a day was a pattern that prevented us from col-lapsing in total fatigue. Since our unknown destination was remote, it was apparent the Japs needed to keep us alive or face the likelihood of carrying the supplies themselves. On the second or third day out, a pack animal collapsed and was shot and butchered, and its meat became part of our diet for the next few days. Once in a while, I'd look up and see the tropical green hills and jungles blending into mountains and admire the beautiful landscape, wondering where the hell we were heading.

When the light of day was gone, our contingent stopped for the day. Usually a small field or a clearing off the trails is where we would rest for the night. We were allowed to cluster in groups while the Nips started a fire, rattled their pots, and cooked food. Once they got their fill, we were lined up, and each of us got slopped a small can of their leftovers. We only got one meal a day, and it was always a sticky mush of rice with fish or some kind of meat, blended with specks of green or yellow vegetables. The portion was more than we got at Camp O'Donnell, but nobody was going to get fat from the meager portions we were allowed. At night, Jap guards sometimes mingled among the prisoners. Some tried out the few words of English they knew, and others simply tormented us, but for the most part they stayed in their own group. After eating, we were allowed to build small campfires and use our tin cans of water blended with roots in an attempt to make tea. Sometimes our little experiments resulted in brews that almost tasted like tea, but usually our concoctions tasted like roots. Nobody had tobacco, so we used bits of paper and rolled up dried leaves or grass to smoke. The blends produced nasty smoke and a terrible taste, but they at least brought back memories of good American cigarettes. Talk at the end of the day was short-lived because the march was so exhausting, and we all knew rest was important if we were going to survive the next day's hike. Before sunrise we were roused to our feet and rigged up with our loads, and the damned march began anew. It was often a struggle from minute to minute to stay upright, especially when our path was loose gravel or roots. As I learned during the march out of Bataan, I sucked on pebbles to stave off the extreme thirst. All day long, it was one step more and then another. I kept my eyes looking down to prevent stumbling and day-dreamed of home, Kakie, and good food. And I prayed.

In the first hours each morning, mist or fog kept things a bit cooler, but it didn't take long for the sun to turn us into sweaty and stinky hogs. Quick rain showers offered a few minutes of relief but also threatened slips and falls when the ground got slippery. Even with rest stops, a few men collapsed and could not or would not get up. I witnessed several being bay-oneted where they fell. A few others punched guards, and it was their final act of defiance as they were immediately killed. Such memories of buddies suffering and dying will never go away. However, in all fairness, a few guards did help men along the way. But it was probably because they knew if too many of their slaves were lost, they would be forced to carry the loads. Like the death march, I believe some of our men grew so frustrated and hopeless they chose suicide over the constant misery. By this time, I had seen so much suffering and death I refused to judge individuals. I trusted and prayed upon death that God would take them into his loving arms and give them a place in paradise. Despite trading off our loads, many were suffering bruises and cuts from the metal-edged ammo boxes. We used rags to cushion the rub spots but without much success.

About the third day, Tom and Red began mumbling about running off. By this time, we were in the mountains, and somebody who knew the local geography said we were getting close to Bontoc. My buddies were increasingly convinced that every single man would eventually die from this never-ending march. They were confident the Japs would work us to death and then get some new suckers to haul their stuff. Honestly, I didn't like the idea of escape because I knew it would be damn near impossible to outrun bullets, and none of us knew where the hell to go if we were lucky enough to escape bullets and trench mortar shells. I offered my opinion, but it soon became apparent that Tom, Steve, and Red were ready to escape when the best opportunity presented itself. While I felt our best chances to survive might be to stick it out, hoping guerrillas or McArthur would soon liberate us, in my heart I knew whatever my buddies decided, I would grudgingly follow along.

As best I can remember, it was the sixth night of our forced march that I nearly got myself killed. Looking back, I did something really stupid, but at the time it was a moment I boldly stood up to one of the terrible guards. On that particular evening, my buddies and I were sitting around our little fire when a goofy-looking black duck casually waddled by. I instantly grabbed it, wrung its neck, and began plucking its feathers, telling the boys we were going to get a little fresh meat. As I yanked the feathers out, Tom gathered a few sticks so we could roast the little duck. Then, out of the darkness, a guard approached and grunted something while motioning me to stand up and hand over the duck. I guess something in me snapped at that moment, and I decided not to hand it over. I felt I had caught it, and it was mine. The sentry had other ideas, however, and a dangerous ordeal began. He motioned again for me to surrender my catch and pointed his bayonet straight at my chest. Now this was serious, and as my anger over the situation rose, I shouted no, no, no. The guard knew the English word *no* and thrust his bayonet at me. I jumped away and became scared but steadfast in my resistance.

At first my guys laughed at my predicament, but realizing the danger, they shouted that I hand over the duck, but I refused. The guard then swung the butt of his rifle at me, which hit me squarely in my chest and knocked me flat on my ass. He again signaled me to give him the duck. Slightly winded but not bloodied, I jumped to my feet, and we began a frightening dance. The guard was now pissed and began to jab his bayonet at me, but I jumped to the left and then to the right to avoid his dangerous thrusts. By now my buddies were begging me to quit. Also, a few other guards had gathered around and began teasing and cheering their buddy. His assault continued, and I fell a few more times, but either my quickness or luck was on my side, and I never got stabbed.

This confrontation continued for ten or fifteen minutes, and I got tired and thought I might actually die, but for some strange reason I decided not to give up my duck. The scene got noisy and weird, as the Jap guards were now laughing and clapping while my buddies were pleading with me to give up the bayonet dance. In all the confusion, I began to lose my balance and fell a few more times, and I was surprised the guard didn't drive his long bayonet straight through me. The guard's face twisted into a big grin as he stood over me one time. I began to wonder if he really wanted my duck or just a chance to torture a defenseless prisoner. Evidently all the noise had roused everyone, including a Japanese officer. He was young, and once on the scene, he shouted orders that quieted his sentries and placed my attacker at attention. In good English he asked me for an explanation for the commotion. I breathlessly sputtered that I had killed a duck for food, and his bastard guard was trying to take it away. The officer wheeled around and faced his guard, shouted at him, and after a bunch of bowing, the guard disappeared. The officer then got right in my face and yelled that I should never refer to any of his soldiers with the ugly term *bastard*. His voice then lowered, and he told me I had caught the duck so it was mine to keep, and furthermore his guard was wrong to take it away.

I was astounded and obviously relieved at the outcome. In hindsight the officer was fair and may have saved my life. To this day, I wonder why I defied an armed guard over a miserable little duck. Sometimes I think after months of experiencing and witnessing defeat and inhumane treatment from the enemy, frustration overruled my common sense. My experience with rage also helped me better understand why some men boiled over in such anger and got themselves killed. In a silent prayer, I thanked God for his mercy in allowing me to survive. My buddies cooked the duck and enjoyed the fresh meat, but I had little appetite after the struggle and only chewed a few tidbits. For a long time thereafter, Tom and the others, who witnessed the whole affair, teased me about what they called "my dance for dinner." It was a scary dance escaping a dangerous bayonet.

The daily marches in the sweltering heat continued. A few more men fell away and were executed where they stumbled. Even though we switched loads, Tom's back and shoulders continued to be a mess of sores and infection. He frequently got quiet and glum and more easily fatigued than the normal buddy I had grown to know. Increasingly, I agreed with the others that this slave-labor detail would probably end up killing us all. We agreed the daily exertion of bearing a heavy load in the oppressive heat could eventually put us all in a grave. The men in our detail were getting weaker every day, and I wondered what would happen next if we reached the end of this forced march. Would our caravan simply walk out of the mountains and begin another journey laden with boxes and bags to other isolated Jap outposts, or would we be returned to Camp O'Donnell? It seemed to me surviving as pack animals would only get us involved in another forced march or something worse. Every night as the four of us rested in the grass staring at the stars, more of our whispered talk turned to escape. We all realized escape was a terrible risk but agreed surviving this march was just as risky. Our talk eventually boiled down to picking the right place and right time, and praying the Lord would safely guide us. Since many Filipinos outright despised the Japanese, we felt they might offer us some help. The chance of hooking up with Filipino and American guerillas seemed possible if we busted away from this miserable detail. We decided whatever happened, we would all stick together in our effort. Finally, we swore to not discuss our plans with other prisoners as some might be desperate or scared enough to rat us out.

We concluded our best chance for escape would be at night when just a few guards patrolled our encampment. Each evening our march would end near sunset, which gave the Japs enough light to get chow together, set up their overnight camp, and post the perimeter with guards. Prisoners would be given a small area to unstrap their loads, mingle, and rest.

Once we got our meal for the day, we could either stretch out to sleep or build small fires and talk. Conversations were always short-lived since total exhaustion made sleep more important than chitchat. The locations where we stopped varied depending upon the terrain. Some nights our march stopped at small fields along the trail, rocky overhangs, or near streams or small lakes. The Jap commander seemed to favor an overnight place near water. I think he liked being near water because it provided his troops with an easy source for cooking and bathing. Once in a while, a few of the Nips would skinny-dip and bathe once the night's encampment was secured. If we attempted to run off, we knew that quickly getting to cover was a critical element in escaping their guns and mortars. Also, we calculated our captors would attempt to quickly capture or kill us but probably not deploy too many troops for too long in pursuit.

One night we were camped near a swift river. Our side of the river was a slight hill sloping down from a steep mountain to the stream. On the other side of the river, there was an embankment of loose rocks and orange clay leading up to stands of bamboo and dense jungle. After eating, the four of us were preparing to sleep when a guard brought us a few dozen jangling mess kits. He pointed to a sandy spot along the river and ordered us to clean the mess gear. So off we trudged, and without a word, I think we realized this might be our chance. As we dipped the utensils in the water, we observed two guards walking a straight line along the riverbank. They would march off in opposite directions, then reverse their walk, and meet each other briefly before repeating their patrol. When the guards were farthest apart, they were several hundred yards away from each other and briefly had their backs to us. Also, the other Japs up the hill were generally lying around and not watching us or the sentries. We decided, with a few exchanged words and nods, to make our move when the sentries were at the far ends of their patrol. We quietly slid into the water and, feeling the current, began to swim like hell. After two or three minutes, a guard evidently saw our bobbing heads and began firing and screaming. Luckily the stream had a strong current, so without too much effort, we found ourselves swiftly moving down the river. I think the chilly mountain water actually gave us fresh energy as we quickly moved farther away from the campsite and all the shouting. Fortunately, we distanced ourselves from their rifle fire but didn't slow our swimming. Then we heard automatic guns and the concussion of the mortars exploding nearby in the water. Although we could hear the ping of bullets and boom of the mortars, nobody was hit. Some of the mortar rounds were ripping up the bushes and trees along the bank. The pull of the stream became overpowering a few times, and I began to worry more about drowning than getting shot. Despite our exertion, the excitement of the moment kept us all afloat as we bobbed up and down.

After moving through several bends in the river, it became dark, and even though the sounds of gunfire and mortars continued, I felt we had made a clean escape. After tumbling over rocks in one choppy area of rapids, we headed for a place to come ashore on the riverbank opposite the campsite. The four of us scrambled up an embankment of twisted roots, and a few yards later, we hid ourselves in a jumble of underbrush. The spot was well camouflaged from the river. Since the Japs had no boats, and we figured they wouldn't swim after us, we felt safe for the moment. Though winded, we quietly congratulated ourselves and were pretty hopped up that we had succeeded in our escape. By this time, it was pitch dark, and the sounds of gunfire were now distant. We needed rest so we hunkered down in the dirt. After a while the recoil of rifles and mortar rounds stopped and things got quiet, so we headed for higher ground. The moonlight was dim because of clouds and a few brief downpours. We blindly scampered through slippery clay and vines until we reached a flat area well above the river. We stumbled upon a low wooden structure in which we huddled together. Once inside we heard a few grunts and chased away several resident pigs. We spent our first night of freedom in a nasty pig sty, but for the first time in many months slept as free men. I think our escape occurred somewhere between Bontoc and Conner in the Kalinga, Apayao, or Cagayan Province region.

On our first morning of freedom, we were roused by thunder and lightning. Also, in the dim light we viewed our resting place, and it was a stinky and muddy hovel. Nonetheless, we awoke happy as larks realizing, at least for the moment, we were free from the enemy and our slave-labor detail. Even with no earthly idea of where to go or what we could find to eat, we were a giddy foursome though thoroughly encrusted in pig poop and mud. The hogs we displaced stood around grunting as we tried to decide our next move. We briefly discussed what a fine meal one of the porkers might provide, but having no means to kill, butcher, or cook anything, they escaped our menu. Also, if we dared make a fire to cook anything, it would be stupid and likely signal enemy patrols. We found an outcropping of rocks and peeked from high above the river where we could see the water and, in the distance, the camp from which we had escaped. It looked as though the prisoners had been assembled and rigged with their loads and were beginning their march. It all looked normal, but we knew the Japs were mad as hell over our escape and had possibly sent out a few soldiers to hunt us down. With this in mind, we decided our best plan would be to further distance ourselves from the river. Setting out from the flatland of our night's rest, we walked into dense jungle and areas full of tall cogon grass and bamboo. Without a map, supplies, food, or any idea where we were heading, we walked. Steve, Tom, Red, and I were ragged and filthy but liberated guys now tromping along and joking about the delicious bacon and pork chops we had just left behind.

After about an hour, we stopped for a rest. While talking about our plans, nobody noticed two brown, almost-naked natives who instantly appeared. Both carried long bamboo poles tipped with bayonet blades, and one had a bow and a bundle of arrows strapped across his back. Neither was smiling.

VII

Guerrilla Action –
Betrayal - Badang

Facing two healthy, unsmiling natives, we nervously awaited their next words or actions. Tom, Red, Steve, and I were
tired, hungry, and without weapons. Obviously, this encounter could turn bad if they considered us their enemies. Also,
we had no knowledge of Tagalog to communicate. I knew
the Japs were all over the countryside and had recruited
or intimidated many locals as bounty hunters to round up
American and Filipino soldiers. It was a known fact that
the Nips used threats, torture, executions, and even rape as
means to secure support and aid from natives. As they slowly looked us over and exchanged words, I wondered if they
were headhunters sizing us up as trophies or merely curious.
Back at Camp O'Donnell, someone told me an American's
head or dog tags could earn a reward. As we nervously stood
facing them, one of the men broke the silence and uttered
"Joe" to his buddy. Tom quickly repeated Joe and pointed
to each of us as Joe, Joe, and Joe. This response changed
their scowls into grins, and they giggled and repeated Joe

a few more times to each other. Finally, they extended their hands and gave each of us a handshake and a slap on the back. Then they motioned us to follow them. While it was only a few minutes, the early morning encounter seemed like an hour. We were defenseless and only hours after escape from the slave-labor gang, so things could have gone deadly. However, *Joe* was the magic word, and we were lucky.

We followed them for about an hour, and I was relieved our discovery by the now-smiling natives might end well. We stopped at a clearing near several thatched huts, which were well camouflaged in a cluster of bamboo. They motioned us to enter a hut, and once inside they exchanged words that included *Joe* to a crouched old couple. The old couple smiled, and the woman offered each of us a large leaf full of something. She signaled us to eat, and we devoured the food, which was a pasty blend of spicy rice and fish. It tasted mighty good, and being very hungry, we all gobbled up their offering like starving hound dogs. The food perked us up, and Tom patted the old lady on the head and shoulders, but she didn't understand his advances and shrunk away. I'm sure he was flirting with the old lady, trying to get another leaf full of chow, but she didn't oblige. About the only word the couple and our captors exchanged occasionally in their talking was *Joe* this and that. After sitting for a while, the old man produced gourds filled with water and directed us to follow the natives we first encountered. Before leaving, I noticed a nearly black ball hanging in a corner, and I'm sure it was a shrunken head. Perhaps in his younger days the old man was a warrior. We bowed and thanked the old folks and exchanged hugs and handshakes. We found out later the friendly Filipinos we encountered were indeed part of a headhunting clan but obviously not interested in our heads.

With our two guides, we hiked another three or four hours farther into the densely forested highlands. As usual the day was another scorcher full of flies and mosquitoes. However, the uphill climb along narrow ridges and paths didn't seem so bad since we were farther away from the Japs and those terrible loads strapped to our backs. We figured our location was deep in Kalinga Province, and we were moving through the mountains and valleys of the Cagayan area. This was an area in the northern part of Luzon Island. The mountain provinces of Kalinga, Ifugao, and Apayao were rugged places full of thick jungles and mountains with a sparse population scattered throughout the hills and valleys. I believe the Japanese saw little military need for a heavy presence here, and our detail of human pack animals was likely heading to their isolated outposts in the region. As we trekked along, the hike again reminded me of my experiences with the CCC camp, tromping through the highlands of West Virginia. Remembering all the hard work and fun I enjoyed with those boys and the wild local women occupied my thoughts as we marched along. Late in the day, our guides delivered us to a guerrilla camp hidden in a small valley.

At the outpost we were met by an American, who introduced himself as a cavalry captain. He wore no captain's bars, and what was left of his uniform was ragged but not as bad as our clothes. None of the officers we met wore insignias of their rank because in the field the badge of an officer made one a priority target for snipers. Unfortunately, I've forgotten all of their names, but the captain we first met proved to be a good and fair leader in the coming weeks. His name was Swick. We briefly exchanged our stories of escape and imprisonment, and the awful things we had witnessed and experienced. He told us we were damn lucky to break away from the labor detail and said he had heard of few such escapes. His experiences were similar to ours. Like us, he had been at Bataan during the final days before surrender, but he and several buddies successfully escaped before the surrender and the death march began. They spent weeks dodging Japs and steadily moving north, feeling their best chances would be to hide in the mountains. He told us we had arrived at a fairly safe place since only small Japanese patrols and possibly a garrison were in the area. He advised us to exercise extreme caution in all our activities as we ventured away from the camp. He insisted our number one job was to first survive and then join him and his guerrillas in fighting the Japs.

There were far more Filipino soldiers and civilian runners in our midst. Runners were men who ran from place to place gathering information about enemy locations and determining the loyalty of barrio chiefs. Most of the men we encountered carried old rifles. The captain informed us that Corregidor had fallen, and all US forces in the Philippines had officially surrendered to the Japs. The four of us were ordered to rest and build ourselves a place to sleep. We were further directed to report in a few days and get details about our assignment. We gathered some canvas, rope, and bamboo poles and rigged a lean-to big enough to sleep in and not get too wet from the daily afternoon thunderstorms. Chow at the camp primarily consisted of rice and available vegetables. Sometimes we received fruit and enjoyed chunks of meat or fish with our rice. The food came from locals or guys in the camp who snared or trapped small animals and birds. It was much better food than the crap we got served as prisoners. We also had coffee and a local tobacco that wasn't as nasty as the mess we had rolled and puffed while lugging cargo. Although I heard occasional gunfire in the distance, the camp seemed a safe and isolated place. The four of us agreed we were lucky to have been rounded up by pro-American natives and land at this camp.

After a few days, Captain Swick called us to his hutch and told us to split into two squads because two-man squads were quieter and thus harder to detect. Naturally, Tom and I became one squad while Steve and Red became the other team. Tom and I were assigned a runner named Lakewood. He was a Filipino and former member of the constabulary. He spoke bamboo English and would serve as our translator and guide. Our assignment was to move along the trails and between the barrios and collect information on the Japs. Lakewood would hike ahead of us to check out the presence of enemy patrols before we entered any settlements. He would then hustle from place to place and back to camp with any useful intelligence. His job was to be our runner and scout. Lakewood wore civilian clothes to blend in with other Filipinos and have a better chance of surviving any encounters with the Japs. Tom and I were issued old rifles and some ammo but were told to avoid using our guns or contacting the enemy unless we had no other choice. It was understood that the enemy patrols were larger and better equipped than our squads, and our primary job was to gather intelligence about enemy activities and the loyalty of local barrio chieftains. While most Filipinos favored the Allies, we were warned that spies, traitors, and informants were among the natives. It was no secret that villagers were rewarded, intimidated, and threatened by the Japanese to inform on Americans. Lakewood was charged with securing us food and shelter in the friendly barrios and teaching us about conditions and living in the jungles and mountains.

With few supplies and food, the three of us began moving along the trails from local village to village. Lakewood had a good knowledge of the local territory, and we had a few roughly drawn maps. There seemed to be a network of runners and soldiers infiltrating the area, and we sometimes encountered other squads. Once Lakewood checked things out, we entered barrios, and a few times we received friendly welcomes, food, and a dry place to sleep. Many little clusters of huts were scattered around the area. If Lakewood knew a village had a spy or headman favoring the Nips, we would station ourselves outside the barrio. We carefully proceeded along the trails, listening for any sounds of a Jap patrol. Many of the known and hidden trails were extremely dense with hanging vines and underbrush. On several occasions we could hear Japs talking and thrashing about but never see them. We listened and learned from our friendly sources the size of Jap patrols, where and when they were last seen, and other bits of information. Lakewood and other runners understood some Japanese, and this helped us in gathering bits of intelligence. We never wrote anything down and usually communicated our findings when we reported to an officer at the base camp. Tom and I returned to camp once or twice a week and got debriefed about the things we had heard, seen, or suspected.

After a few weeks, our camp acquired several cranky phones that could be used in the field to call the base or other squads out on the trails. The crankies got their name from a cranking handle that gave the units power but were sometimes unreliable. While in the field, Lakewood and other natives taught us quite a bit about the right berries, seeds, nuts, and grubs to eat and which ones to avoid touching or eating. Frequently wading through streams, we quickly realized the nuisance of leeches and the good taste of crayfish. We were forbidden to use fire for cooking except when fog or mist filled the air. Smoke was an obvious signal to our enemy, and we even curtailed smoking except when fog was present. Naturally, out in the bush we encountered snakes of all sizes and colors squirming across the trail or hanging overhead. Once a damn boa plopped down on me from a limb, and I wrestled like hell to keep the monster from choking me while Tom and Lakewood chuckled. The nonpoisonous snakes were as dangerous as the poisonous ones because a big boa constrictor or python could squeeze your life away in a few minutes. Throughout these hills there were also small deer, speedy lizards, wild pigs, noisy monkeys, rats, huge spiders, birds, and of course bugs. We did our best to avoid leeches, but they hung from bushes and filled the creeks and streams just waiting to grab hold and suck blood.

After a few weeks of patrols, a major called me aside one day and asked my military rank. I told him I had been a private since joining the army and arriving at Clark Field. He smiled and told me I was doing an excellent job. He then gave me a handwritten order promoting me to buck sergeant. I thought it was a nice gesture, but since we weren't getting pay in the guerrilla outfit, I didn't think it was such a big deal. The only money we regularly got in the Philippines was pesos and military script, which we used for food, smokes, and other things. However, after our surrender at Bataan, money became useless. Because we were far away from cities or towns, money became obsolete, and we got necessary things at our camp by trading with local people. Evidently word of my promotion spread quickly, and Tom, along with others, soon teased me about becoming a buck sergeant. They spent days greeting me with exaggerated salutes and bows. The major and captain assured me I deserved the field promotion because I was a good leader, used common sense, and treated others fairly. I had no experience or training to be a sergeant but trusted their words and advice.

After my promotion, I was assigned a few more runners, and our patrols lasted a little longer and stretched farther into the countryside. I was also given a new responsibility to dispose of traitors or any captured Japs we encountered. Frankly, I didn't like the idea of executing anybody and hoped not to exercise that duty. I believed God's commandment about killing, but I also knew the dog-eat-dog nature of war and the cruelty of the enemy. While I relished the idea of getting revenge on the devils who had tortured and killed my buddies and fellow soldiers, a small voice inside warned me otherwise. My order was clear, and unless a prisoner was a Jap officer or soldier who spoke English, it was my new responsibility to bury them. I certainly understood we had no extra food or jail for prisoners, so when a Nip or Filipino turncoat was caught, and after hearing the evidence, I had to be judge, jury, and executioner. Reluctantly I began to order my runners to do the killing and burying when a traitor or Jap soldier was caught. I gave specific instructions to march the guilty individuals down a trail, have them dig their own graves, and then have my men kill them. I had to be very careful on several counts. First, we didn't have much ammo, and without knowing the location of other Japs, we didn't want to be noisy and draw attention to our location. Next, we told our runners to deliver a clean kill without torture and without gunfire. A bolo chop to the jugular or head clubbing was quiet and usually resulted in a quick death. However, many Filipinos who had family members tortured or killed by the Japs wanted revenge, and it took a while before I understood this.

I vividly remember one time we caught a Filipino traitor who had gotten Colonel Folksom killed. This man worked with the colonel but unexpectedly told the Japs everything they needed to know to ambush and kill him. The colonel was a hell of a leader, and the Japs placed a large bounty on his capture or killing. His traitor turned out to be a local man named Sexto Felliciano. Sexto was educated, spoke good English, and had been a trusted aide for several other American officers. I will never forget his name or face. Sexto admitted to leading the Japs to Folksom, but he begged for mercy and wept. He pleaded that he had a wife and three little children, and for their sake, he shouldn't have to die. This made me angry, and I told Sexto that Colonel Folksom also had a wife and children. I dismissed his plea for mercy, and he got very quiet and hung his head. I ordered three of my Filipino scouts to take Sexto a few hundred yards down the trail and waste him. They took several hours to get the job done, and a week or so later, I noticed the trio laughing like hyenas and tossing around a piece of bone. I asked one of the boys, named Gothas, about the piece of bone. After some plodding, he admitted it was part of Sexto Felliciano's skull. Unbeknownst to me, Gothas and his pals had tortured and beheaded Sexto. At least one of the three was from a tribe of headhunters, and the piece of skull became their trophy. The incident sickened me, not because Sexto didn't deserve his punishment but because of the torture and mutilation of his body. I hated the cruelty of unnecessary torture and never got used to it, whether the cruelty was shown by the Japs, Americans, or Filipinos. After the Sexto Felliciano incident, I began to witness every execution to ensure there was no torture. Decades later, I occasionally have bad dreams and will probably never forget the case of Sexto Felliciano. He was the first man I ordered to be executed.

Moving around the mountains and jungles, Tom and I continued to learn a lot from Lakewood and other runners, in addition to the local people, about the various tribes and their ways of life. They also taught us how to set snares to catch small critters and birds. We were also given guidance on the best ways to track and kill deer and wild boar using spears and bows. Of course, fresh killed meat did not last long in the tropics, so we always shared our food with the locals when we bagged a large animal. In return the grateful Filipinos gave us water from their wells, as well as rice, tobacco, and vegetables. Most importantly they kept our whereabouts secret. I also got pretty good at spearing fish in the streams. One old man showed me a berry that when squashed and scattered into a pond or creek would temporarily stun fish, which made them easy to scoop up. A small man from a Negrito village made me a bow and several arrows. Although his bow was taller than he was, he was an excellent shot. Several times I saw him shoot small monkeys perched high in trees. I used and practiced with my bow but never got as good as this Negrito tribesman. This tribe of small people stood only four to four-and-a-half feet tall, were said to be headhunters, and carried a reputation as fierce warriors. They showed Tom and I which insects could be safely eaten raw or cooked. I remember one particular large, white caterpillar found in dead trees that amazingly tasted as sweet as candy.

After a few months tromping around, our shoes finally fell apart, and Tom and I began running around shoeless. The soles of our feet got tough, and we were scooting around the jungles as easily as the natives. Naturally bugs of every size and color were everywhere and constantly biting. We had no netting so the mosquitoes and bugs got to us, especially when we slept. After rainstorms and down in swampy areas, the bugs became thick black clouds of buzzing and biting. The mosquitoes delivered the biggest and nastiest sting, which often resulted in big welts. We used rags and old blankets as coverings when we slept, but they never kept the bugs away. And wading through streams and heavy brush, we constantly encountered leeches. The little buggers attached themselves to any exposed flesh and with a little prick began drawing blood. Their initial attachment did not hurt as much as their removal. There were little black and dark-green vampires, and like ticks they lived off blood. I remember those jungle days and nights and the unusual things we saw, but especially the creatures ever ready to bite or eat me.

After several months, our captain called us together and told us a Jap garrison was getting closer to our location; the guerrilla camp had to be disbanded and moved. He gave us rough maps pointing to a location farther in the mountains that he felt would be a safer place for our operations. Except for the guns, ammo, radios, and small equipment, he ordered all the heavy stuff to be destroyed. Importantly, he wanted most of us to move in teams of two or three with our runners to our new location. He insisted small squads would have a better chance of moving quickly and quietly over the terrain while evading the enemy. Tom and I asked Lakewood to be our runner, and he agreed. Of the runners we had encountered, Lakewood had proven to be the most loyal and reliable of the bunch. He knew the trails and some barrio leaders, and despite having a wife and little kids, he never complained about the separation from his family. We moved out early the morning after our new orders were announced. We began moving from hamlet to hamlet, following the map. In one barrio near the town of Conner, Lakewood secured a caballo, which is a small pony. Tom and I rode and used the little thing to carry our supplies for a few weeks. It saved us a lot of walking, but we gave it up in a village when the poor animal began to whine and groan too much. We realized it was getting weak and became concerned that its moaning might tip off our location to an enemy patrol. As we moved from barrio to barrio, some locals we encountered were friendly while others were hostile. We never knew which tribes were headhunters, but we saw shrunken heads proudly displayed in some huts we visited.

One day we got lost, and even Lakewood was unsure of our location or the right track to follow. We came upon a tiny village in a deep valley that was surrounded by large hills and seemed a good isolated spot for us to spend a few days. We sheltered outside the hamlet while Lakewood entered the barrio to determine their loyalties and seek information to get us back on the right track. Lakewood returned and told us the chief man was pro-American, so Tom and I entered the barrio, and the people greeted us as friends. They put us up in a thatched hut standing on stout bamboo poles. We were given food and a local drink, which tasted of coconut milk but had a good kick. As we tried to figure our location, our stay stretched from days to weeks, and I recall a funny and odd incident involving Tom and a chubby local girl named Rosa. Somehow Tom hooked up with this little woman and her three little kids. Her husband had either run off or joined some guerrilla outfit, so Tom moved in with her and her children. She spoke a little bamboo English and seemed a nice enough young woman. Tom teased and played with the children, and she began following him around like a guide dog. She also cleaned his clothes, shaved him, fed him, and cut his hair. After a while Tom announced he was going to marry the girl, and I thought he was joking since he was engaged to Fran back home. But he insisted it would be okay since we were in a war zone, and he asked me for help to get a dowry. Seems Rosa's father agreed to the marriage but insisted on a gift from Tom to seal the deal. I didn't have anything to offer, and Tom rummaged around a few days trying to find a suitable gift for the father.

One day I was surprised when the marriage ceremony proceeded, and many villagers assembled in the town square. The village headman officiated, and Tom asked that I be his best man. With many looking on, a village leader officiated, chanted a few words, and tapped the bride and groom on the head with a beautiful bunch of feathers while everyone cheered. With this the marriage was done, and a wedding party began and grew into a grand affair of dancing, singing, and laughing. We all enjoyed a feast and had a gay old time. While the marriage seemed crazy, from all appearances it seemed a good match for Rosa and her children with Tom. Later, when I couldn't find the rosary beads given me by the Jesuit, Tom confessed he had swiped the beads to satisfy the need to provide Rosa's father with a dowry gift. I forgave Tom for his theft, and ironically, I think most of the villagers were pagans.

After another week or so, Lakewood and several local men thought they knew of a trail which would get us unlost and headed in the right direction to our new guerrilla post. On the morning we left the village, Rosa and her kids followed Tom like he was a father goose. After about a mile, Tom shooed them away amid a lot of goodbye hugs, tears, and kisses. Tom didn't talk much about his wife and kids, but in my opinion, it was one of his wackiest stunts. Including Tom's antics, the time we spent in this particular village provided a good and necessary rest. After several days of hiking, Lakewood found us a place to rest right outside of a small settlement. He wasn't sure if the barrio was controlled by the Japs, so we quietly sheltered for the night in a dark hut. The hut was grounded near a marsh, and we quickly realized the place was full of rats. So, our first job was to chase out the vermin. Lakewood woke us before the sun rose, whispered a Jap patrol was nearby, and motioned us to move quickly. We double-timed into the nearby jungles as quietly as possible. As we escaped, the enemy was so close we could hear them talking as we crawled and quickly scrambled away. On another occasion, we came upon an abandoned hut on stilts standing in a clearing all by itself. From behind some boulders, we watched it a few days before we decided it was safe. With two new runners, we made this hut our base for a few days. After scouting the territory, which was evidently controlled by the Japs, we carefully returned to the hut to sleep. One morning before the sun rose, we were rudely awakened by ungodly screaming and several bursts of gunfire. Instantly, we dove headlong out of the hut, tumbled into the mud, and ran like hell. Although we grabbed our guns, ammo, and a few supplies, we forgot our new map and compass. Stumbling and running through the darkness and brush, we escaped the ambush. After rushing away from the rifle fire for at least an hour, we felt safe enough to stop and rest.

When we collapsed just off a dusty trail, our clothes were torn by thorns, and our arms and legs were bloodied. As we caught our breath, we soon realized one of our new runners named Peter was missing. I remember he jumped out of the hut with us and was either shot or captured during our run. Peter was a teenager and cousin to several other runners we had known, and he was a nice kid. Days later, we heard he had been wounded, captured, and tortured. A family member found his mutilated body in a ditch. Tom and I were convinced someone tipped off the Japs, or they were lucky to discover our hideout. Increasingly, the Japanese surprised our small squad, and we ended up scatting into the jungle for cover. We had some awfully close calls, and their patrols now seemed to be everywhere. From friendly natives we got reports of guerrillas getting captured, so I decided to no longer use any footpaths or marked trails. Without our map, we were lost again, and Lakewood thought our best course was to move in a northerly direction deeper into the mountain provinces. Our goal was to find our new camp or any guerrilla base. Our extended travels took us through endless fields of chest-high cogon grass, prickly underbrush, swamps, and jungles, plus on exhausting climbs over rocks and boulders. The razor-sharp grasses and needled bushes tore at our clothes and left more scratches. Every night we sought fresh water to hydrate ourselves and clean our wounds. I knew untreated scrapes, if infected, could be as deadly as a cobra bite or bullet.

As the grueling days passed, it became more difficult to find barrios that would help us with water, food, or information. Even with our limited knowledge of living off the land and help from Lakewood, finding sufficient food and water became a tricky proposition. As we eventually lost contact with other runners, I felt our overall situation was getting worse. Then, one afternoon, we spotted a lean-to set among some big rocks high above a barrio. We watched it for a few hours, and after Lakewood checked it out, Tom and I moved in at sunset. Exhausted, we found dry spaces to get some sleep. The next morning, I told Lakewood to make his way down to the barrio and size things up. He understood his job and moved out in hopes of finding a safe hamlet to travel through and possibly get information to find our way. Usually Lakewood would return within a few hours with information or news, but the day passed, and he didn't come back. Nervously, we waited two more days, but he didn't return. Tom and I began to think Lakewood might have been captured or killed. We trusted him, and after months of companionship, he had proven to be a loyal and hardworking runner and friend. We didn't have binoculars, and the hamlet was too far away to clearly see anything, so we decided to stay put, anticipating

Lakewood would eventually show up. If he didn't return, we knew we'd have to move out on our own because staying in the same place too long increased our chance of a Jap patrol discovering us. Early on about the fifth or sixth morning, we decided to leave, feeling Lakewood had fallen into enemy hands or worse. I told Tom to gather up our gear, and I climbed boulders far above our hut to get some fresh water and a few crayfish from a little mountain stream we had discovered. After getting a few crawdads and two canteens of water, I prepared to descend and join Tom for our departure. When I heard high-pitched shouting, I peeked over the rocks at a horrifying scene that damn near broke my heart.

Looking down, I saw four Japs had captured Tom and collected our rifles. They were looking all around, realizing that two guns probably meant two men. I froze in place and watched as the soldiers hollered at each other, tied Tom's hands, kicked him, and then fitted a rope around his neck. Tom stood still and didn't say a word as best as I could see. I was in a hopeless situation and watched as the bastards shoved Tom and roughly yanked at the rope around his neck as they pulled him down a path. I watched, but they soon disappeared into the woods. Tom never looked back in my direction, and I knew he would die before he'd tell them my whereabouts. At that moment, I realized Tom was probably a goner. From our meeting at Fort Belvoir and through all the hell we'd experienced, Tom and I had remained best pals. No matter how bad things looked during our struggles, Tom always had a little joke or smile. He could have easily been the one to dig the crawdads and get water, and then I would have been captured. He was gone, and I was helpless to do anything to help him escape his captors. I had no gun, knife, blanket, gear, or way to start a fire. I had nothing but two canteens full of water and a pocketful of crawdads. I couldn't retrieve anything from the hut because the Japs knew damn well another American soldier was in the area. They would surely be watching and scouting the area to catch me, so I knew my survival depended on how quickly and how far I could distance myself from the enemy. I stared with a sense of disbelief and great sadness as Tom and the Japs slipped out of sight. For the first time, it became clear I was alone without my buddy or a native guide.

To avoid being caught, I knew it was important to move farther into the mountains and away from any settlements or well-worn trails. I quickly and quietly climbed and climbed until my route led me to a small cave. Hunched down there, I chewed the raw crayfish and got sick to my stomach, so I gulped water from my canteen to sate my nausea and thirst. I hid there a few days to get some rest and relief from the heat. Without a source of food or means to cook anything, each night I drew up into a tight ball, trying to be small and invisible, while my empty stomach growled in the total darkness. My thoughts and dreams focused on Tom's fate, Kakie, and what I should do next. Also, I prayed a lot for Tom and for guidance to send me in a safe direction. One night I was awakened by a driving monsoon rain, deafening thunder, and terrific lightning. The storm was so severe I became soaked from rain blowing into the shallow cave. At one point during the worst of the storm, I felt nearby lightning was shooting electricity into the cave as my body tingled.

The next morning, after carefully watching and listening for several hours, I began to cautiously move down the mountain.

After eating a few berries that I knew were safe, I realized it was critical to find clean water and food. I wandered and finally found a little bubbling stream where I drank a bellyful and filled my canteen, hoping the water was safe. I decided to follow the creek, knowing that people usually lived along waterways, and there might be people to help me. By nightfall I hadn't seen a single hut or barrio and felt sick, so I stopped to rest. Under a tree high above the stream, I found a small depression and slid into it, covered myself with nearby palm fronds, and tried to sleep. Instead of rest, I experienced a violent bout of vomiting and diarrhea. Drained of energy, I finally passed out or fell asleep but awoke in the dark with a pounding headache, shakes, and quickly occurring rounds of hot flashes and chills. From the classes at Clark and several other similar incidents, I was sure my symptoms indicated another attack of malaria. Whatever the cause, I was a mess. I remember lying flat on my back, having some scary dreams, and feeling totally drained of energy.

I'm not sure if it was hours or a day or two before I woke up and felt better physically. Though weak and shaky on my feet, I struggled, knowing I must move on and find some help. My balance and strength slowly returned, and I followed the small stream until it emptied into a larger creek. Along the opposite bank, I spotted a small hut sitting all alone and decided to seek its shelter. However, I first crouched down and watched the place for any activity. Late in the day, I saw two men bearing spears enter the hut. After a short visit, they left. I watched a little longer and finally guessed it was a hunting lodge since no other buildings were nearby, and I had seen no other people coming or going. Very carefully, I moved through the creek and ducked into the hut. I looked around for food or anything else. There were a few pieces of dried meat hanging from the ceiling. I also found a burlap sack, a tin can, and a small stone hatchet. I grabbed everything and stuffed it in the burlap bag. Then I quickly moved from the hut to a patch of underbrush back on the opposite side of the stream. Hearing my stomach grumble, I inspected and sniffed the dried meat and spent an hour chewing and hoping it wasn't rotten. The next morning, I felt considerably better.

For the next week or so, I continued my lonely trek staying within sight of the creek's tumbling water. I came upon a few solitary shacks, and when I realized nobody was around, I rushed down and swiped whatever I could find. One time I was able to catch a chicken, and using my hatchet and a piece of swiped flint, I built a small fire and cooked the thing. I continued to eat berries and bugs that I knew were safe. I was barely getting enough nourishment to stay strong for the long hike, which seemed to be going nowhere. I slept on the ground in hidden places, doing my best to stay dry despite the afternoon showers. Every time I heard a nearby bird or animal rustling leaves, I imagined Japs nearby. The loneliness, threatening sounds, and fear of capture caused me to become increasingly nervous, and I couldn't kick worrying about Tom. I began to travel more in the darkness to avoid being spotted, but it was a risky proposition, depending upon the amount of moonlight. I didn't want to step on a slithering snake or fall into a ditch at night, so my movement was slow on the darker nights. Even though I was stealing bits of food here and there from unoccupied huts, I felt my weight was dropping. I was definitely feeling skinnier and struggled to hike from sundown to sunup. My legs became rubbery and weak after only a half-night's march, and I got winded easily, often losing my balance, moving up and down steep grades. After several weeks of being alone and constantly hungry, it became crystal clear to me that I desperately needed help.

One morning I decided that in order to stay alive, I had to take a chance and make contact to get help from someone out in the bush or in a barrio. I hoped they would be anti-Japanese and help me, but there were no guarantees of where their loyalties might lie. I realized if I could find a friendly barrio, there might be food, supplies, and a way to reach a guerrilla camp. I convinced myself that my best option was to find and watch a village, and if I didn't see any Japanese flags or soldiers, I would simply walk into the barrio and ask for help. I still believed most Filipinos were pro-American and peaceful except in places where the Japs had gained sympathizers or spies. I knew straggling into a village could either be my salvation or a fast way to a grave, but I was at my wit's end and had few good choices. Following the stream, I finally spotted a small house, then another, and then a village of ten or fifteen thatched huts. From a distance I watched the barrio and didn't see any military activity so decided to make my move. As I came out of the forest and got on the path leading into the village, a naked boy came out of nowhere and slapped my knees with a stiff switch. After that, the little squirt ran screaming down the lane, and this drew a few men and women out of their huts. They quietly stared as I stumbled along, and it made me feel like a creature from Mars because the people gawked as I passed. Nobody made a sound. Thinking back, I suppose it was a strange sight since my clothes were ragged and stained. I was filthy, probably stinking, and my hair and beard were a nasty, crusty tangle. The burlap sack

I dragged was coming to pieces, and my body was beginning to resemble a Halloween skeleton.

When I got halfway into the hamlet, a man ran up and without a word tied my hands behind my back and pushed me toward a large hut. Inside he forced me to sit on the ground, and he stood guard over me. I tried "Joe" and other bamboo English words and phrases, but he wasn't listening and didn't give any response. Within minutes, a half-dozen older men, some bearing spears, marched in and stood around me in a circle. They looked me up and down and chatted with each other for a few minutes, and then they began to argue. I didn't catch any understandable words as their discussions quickly became a shouting session. I shouted Joe a few times, but nobody acknowledged me. One of the older men stooped down and screamed into my face until I tasted his spit. Having no idea what was happening, I got pretty nervous about the situation. Then they all left the hut, and I was left sitting there with only the unsmiling sentry nearby. A few hours passed, and I looked around the place; to my surprise I noticed several dozen brown balls hung along the walls. I squinted really hard and, upon closer inspection, realized the dark-colored balls were shrunken heads. My sentry noticed me staring at the trophies, nudged me, and shot me a huge, black-toothed grin. The display worried the hell out of me, and I realized the barrio I had chosen to find help was a beehive of headhunters. Another hour dragged on as I thought how in the world I could get out of this mess. The old men finally returned, accompanied by other younger men; some were half-naked, and others wore regular clothes.

Their talking began anew, and it got fiery again with some in the bunch practically going into a frenzy. I decided I had nothing to lose, so I shouted back that I was their friend, an American, and needed help. Nobody seemed to understand my words, and I was beginning to think my goose was cooked. I fervently prayed to myself as two men lifted me and shoved me into a corner. The natives continued to fuss and scream at each other. Confined to a corner of the hut and facing a wall, I resembled a naughty schoolboy. Amid all the confusion and noise, a soft voice behind me whispered, "Sir, they are afraid your presence will draw our enemies, and they want to kill you." The English from the little brown man standing behind me was good, and I was relieved that I might have a translator to plead my case. He asked my name and told me he was Matias Badang, but to call him Badang. I told him my name was Charlie, and I was an American soldier. He told me the argument was whether to take my head and give it to the Japs as a sign of loyalty or allow me to leave their village immediately. The crowd argued on, and finally Badang spoke up and made a speech to the assembly. This quieted the crowd, and I asked him what he told the other men. He told me he promised the elders to take me away and guaranteed I would never return. I felt a little better that at least one person in the room could translate and seemed to be on my side and not want my head. The argument continued, and Matias became a more active participant in the give-and-take. I asked Badang to tell the men I was an advance scout for a large patrol of well-armed Americans. He passed this along, but their response was a combination of hoots and boos. In retrospect, my scraggly appearance didn't convince anyone I was nothing but a lost man. Finally, the oldest guy in the crowd motioned everyone to shut up and made an announcement that ended the session. As everyone filed out of the hut, I asked my translator what was going to happen next. He told me to be quiet and bow to each of the older men as they exited the large room.

When the hut was empty, Badang led me out and walked me down the same trail that had led me into the village. After we walked awhile, he untied my hands. Looking around to ensure our privacy, he whispered that the chief would not take my head if I left the barrio. He added there was a garrison of Jap soldiers a few kilometers away, and the chief was worried what might happen to his people if they found an American in the village. Badang quietly led me up a mountain trail, and we finally sat and rested behind a few huge rocks. I asked him what he was going to do with me, and he admitted he wasn't sure. He acknowledged I was obviously in rough shape and probably wouldn't survive for very long if he simply let me go. However, he repeated his promise to the headman to ensure I would disappear and not return to the village. We sat in silence for a good while, and Badang finally said he had a plan that might work. He explained if he took me up in the mountains, I would be isolated from the barrio as he had pledged and possibly safe from enemy patrols. The place he had in mind was a few kilometers from his hut. By now it was dark, and he asked me to follow him to his cottage so he could gather up a few things and get us a bite to eat. His place was simple but clean, and there he introduced me to his wife and several of his children. At first, they were all wide-eyed and looked scared, but after I winked a few times, they all flashed grins. Carrying a bundle of things, Badang led me back up a trail, which became steep and rocky. A full moon that particular night helped me

ascend the path without falling. Although thoroughly exhausted after the day's drama and hiking, I was energized by
the prospect of a safe hiding place and a new friend, and I
stumbled uphill with a fresh sense of optimism.

When it was fully dark, we finally stopped at a ledge high
above his barrio, which was surrounded and hidden by huge
rocks and tall trees. Without a word, Badang drew his machete and cut some poles from nearby bushes, unfolded a
small piece of thin canvas, and quickly fashioned a shelter
for me. Then he gathered some leaves and laid a bamboo mat
and blanket over them and told me this was my bed. Finally,
he gave me a sack of things to eat wrapped in newspaper
and told me to rest, stay hidden, remain quiet, and not build
a fire. He said he would return in a few days, and as I bowed
and repeated my thanks, he smiled and disappeared. As told,
I rested but couldn't sleep for a long time. I kept wondering
how a bad situation got turned around by this Badang fellow
and wondered why he argued for my life and took responsibility for me. In prayers I thanked God for my good fortune
in encountering this small man of immense kindness, who
chose to rescue me from headhunters and end my endless
wandering. Aside from the usual screeching and squawking
of the night jungle, I finally fell into restful dreams of home.
The food Badang supplied consisted of dried meat, pieces of
fruit, and hard, flat bread made of rice. As he had instructed,
I didn't venture too far from the shelter the next day, except
to get some water that I found in the cavity of a boulder.

When Badang returned, he brought more food, some tobacco, a bolo, several tiny candles, and a tin can. While we
shared food, I asked him the number one question on my

mind. I asked why he argued and intervened on my behalf with the elders of his village and possibly placed himself and his family in danger. Best I can recall, he said, "Sir, I could not let them harm you back there ... What I will do is take care of you until your American friends return." I again asked him why he stuck his neck out, and he continued, "When I was a little boy, Americans came up through the mountains looking for gold ... One of those men used me as his houseboy. I was from a poor family, and this American became a good and fair master and liked me very much. He taught me English, arithmetic, and other things. Sometimes he gave me extra pesos to help my family. When this wonderful man died, I swore I would honor him by helping another American if I ever had a chance. Mr. Charlie, sir, God sent me you to help, and I will." Looking back, I have no doubt I would have died or been buried by the Japs if Badang had not come to my rescue. In addition to convincing the barrio chief to spare my life, he eventually confessed his plan to the village elder, and he kept it secret despite frequent visits from Jap patrols. I knew Badang was taking a big chance since his wife, children, and other villagers might be punished or killed if my presence was revealed. His help was fantastic and may have saved my life. I was damn lucky the day Matias Badang came into my life.

Badang instructed me to never smoke or make a fire unless the air was full of fog or mist because Japanese patrols crossed nearby; any trail of smoke would make them curious and draw their attention. He promised to bring me food whenever he could but said to do my best to find fresh water and things to eat. He reminded me of the dangerous snakes and animals I should avoid. Badang also told me to never come off the mountain into the barrio and never wander far from my hidden location. Before he left, he reached into his sack and pulled out a tattered arithmetic book. He told me it had been a gift from his old American master, and now it was being returned to his new American friend. He said it was the only book he had that was in English. It seemed an odd gift but over the coming months became a valuable asset. First I memorized all the multiplication tables and other rules of algebra and geometry. The little book became a daily way to daydream about my school days and the good times of my youth. After reading and rereading the math book, I began using the pages to roll cigarettes whenever Badang got me a little tobacco and conditions were safe to puff a little smoke. Finally, he promised to change my location if necessary, and then he smiled and gently patted me on the head. I thanked him as he quietly padded away. For a long time after this encounter, I sat quietly until the night sky filled with millions of twinkling stars. Then, out of nowhere, the recent change in my situation hit me like a ton of bricks, and I thanked the Lord. I almost wept over losing Tom, missing my young bride, and being blessed to have this Matias Badang fellow come to my rescue. After this anxiety passed, I prayed for Tom's rescue and peace of mind for my dear Catherine and family. Newly blessed by my meeting with Badang gave me confidence, and I would henceforth make every effort to survive and simply trust the Lord.

Faithful to his word, he returned a few times a week and brought me food, supplies, and whatever news or rumors had floated into his barrio. Soon his neighbor Pio Paned began to visit me occasionally when Badang was off to another village. With their help I moved several more times to different places in the mountains when they felt Japanese patrols were getting too close to my location. For over thirteen months, I lived pretty much alone and only came off the mountain a few times to visit Badang and his family. Needless to say, Badang, Pio, and their families saved my life and recapture from the Japs. During this time, I suffered more attacks of malaria, dysentery, and an increasing level of nervousness. My Filipino friends had no quinine or regular medicine but treated me with their local concoctions. Several times, when I was especially sick and weak, Badang or Pio spent the night with me and applied cool head compresses or an extra blanket when I suffered fevers or chills. While their visits were irregular and only lasted an hour or so, I enjoyed their company and our conversations.

One day Pio explained how their village used a "slash and burn" method of farming. From him I learned that this type of raising crops involved cutting down sections of the forest and setting it on fire. Later I came to understand this method was an ancient technique for raising food. Since they had no modern farm equipment or fertilizers, this procedure every few years gave them fresh soil for their gardens. He told me their main crops were tubers, beans, and lettuce, but no rice. Their land was hilly and incapable of setting up flooded rice paddies, so they acquired rice by trading their vegetables with other villages. They also raised chickens, ducks, and goats and hunted for deer, wild hogs, and other small game. Without refrigerators or electricity, they salted, smoked, and dried most of the meats. Food spoiled quickly in the trop-ics. They also fished the streams for fish and crayfish and speared or gigged frogs and even monitor lizards. Despite the food they supplied, I was always hungry and was sure my weight was dropping. My skin seemed to be shrinking, and my rib bones looked ready to pop out of my chest.

Over my months of solitude, I had many strange and scary experiences. One day I was exploring a little path and encountered a huge snake. It was a boa constrictor with a head bigger than a little human child. It had to be a ten- or fifteen-foot snake. The darn thing crossed right in front of me and lifted its head while its fat forked tongue danced around, sniffing my presence, and then it slithered away. Without a doubt, it was the largest boa constrictor I had ever seen, and it took a long time to cross my path. Luckily, this big serpent had a huge lump in its belly, which indicated it had recently eaten and probably wasn't interested in making a meal of me. I had heard stories of these monsters swallowing deer and even people, and this sucker was easily big enough to eat me. While not poisonous, constrictors kill by wrapping themselves around their prey, choking them to death, and then slowly swallowing their victim whole. I had encountered other large constrictors and pythons dangling from trees, flopping down on me, or slithering nearby, but never one the size of the big boy I ran into that day. It made me nervous, realizing that if a huge boa constrictor snake crawled into my hut while I was asleep, it might easily wrap me in its deathly grip before I could escape and gobble me up.

I found a nice mountain stream near my hut and often went down there. Wading through the cool water to a large rock, I'd relax and enjoy hearing the water swish by. The time I spent sitting on the rocks was peaceful. On one unforgettable night, I was down on the river, lying on my back on my favorite flat boulder and watching the stars twinkle, when I heard a voice. I swear I wasn't high or asleep when I distinctly heard a soft voice say, "Ding Ding, I'm dreaming of you on a rock in a river, and you're looking at the stars." It was scary, but I clearly recognized it as the voice of Catherine's youngest sister, Mary Alice. When I left the states, she was probably only six or seven years old and unable to clearly say my nickname, Dinky, so she called me "Ding Ding." Now Mary Alice was a cute little blond-headed kid, and I loved teasing and playing with her when I lived and visited Catherine and her folks on Lansing Avenue. I don't normally believe in telepathy or any of that stuff, but I considered the voice and words spooky yet a comforting message from home. Ironically, years later after the war when Mary Alice was a teenager, I asked about her vision, and she did remember having dreams of me lying on a rock and watching the stars. This situation will always be a mystery to me.

A frightening thing happened one morning when I awoke in my little hut that I cannot forget. Seems a large cobra was coiled a foot or so from my feet and glaring at me when I awoke. The sucker was sniffing and hissing. I knew, and Badang and others had told me, that cobras attacked and killed many people in the Philippines, and the medicines were practically unavailable, especially in the boondocks. They warned me to avoid the aggressive creature and always steer clear, as they could strike from a good distance. When I saw the cobra, I froze in place and wondered how the heck I could get the thing away from my sleeping area. Before I knew it, the damn thing lunged at me, and my immediate reaction was to throw my blanket over it. It was amazing how fast and how far the cobra flung its body in my direction. Momentarily, the covering confused the creature just long enough for me to tumble halfway out of my hut, brushing against the snake's thick body. It recovered and made a second lunge toward my head, and I swung my walking stick at it. We both missed our target, and this gave me a few more valuable seconds to move quickly out of the hut and then run like hell. Breathlessly, I scampered a few hundred feet thinking the cobra was angry and chasing me. I hid behind a big rock and waited. After a while, I carefully retraced my steps and cautiously looked through my hut and the immediate area. To my good fortune, the cobra was gone.

Speaking of snakes, on another occasion I was digging around the banks of a stream looking for crayfish one afternoon, and a beautifully colored green snake crawled nearby. It was pencil thin but longer than the green snakes back home. Such green snakes were common and harmless at home, so I grabbed the little fellow and allowed it to wrap itself around my hand a few times before it slithered away. A few days later, while talking to Badang, I mentioned my cobra and green snake encounter, and he gasped, telling me the tiny green snake had a deadlier bite than the cobra.

A few months into my hiding, Badang and Pio moved me again to a more remote place. They told me Jap patrols were now visiting their barrio on a regular basis and even checking their huts for any signs of American or Filipino soldiers or POWs. To shield themselves from any undue attention, they told me their visits would decrease, and I would have to find my own food. I also was sternly directed to never get near the village or venture far from my new location. They were afraid I might be spotted by the Japs or betrayed by a local spy. Their visits soon became infrequent, and I had to scrounge for things to eat. Most of the berries, lizards, and grubs I caught were okay to eat, but once in a while I ate something that wasn't so good and got sick to my stomach. On an earlier visit, Badang had helped me fashion a little spear and snare. I used these things to gig lizards and small fish or snare small animals. Carefully using a small campfire or allowing raw meat strips to dry on sun-heated rocks, I supplied myself with things to eat. Over the months, by observing and learning, I had gone native to some extent. I had gathered enough practical information to survive, but as I chewed my unseasoned foods, I still longed for mashed potatoes, pork chops, or fried flounder from the kitchen of Catherine's mother. One day Badang brought me a chunk of freshly cooked meat, and it was the most delicious thing I had eaten in a long time. It tasted like chicken and reminded me of fresh fried chicken. After consuming the tasty meal from his wife, he revealed it was a parrot.

One day, in addition to food, Badang brought me a flat length of wood, some cord made of twisted fibers, and a small knife. He told me we were going to fashion a hunting bow that I could use to hunt small game and birds. I had seen Negritos and other tribes using their bows and arrows with great accuracy, and I even tried their rigs a few times but without much luck. I never considered making or having my own bow and arrows and wholeheartedly joined in the project. For several hours we talked and whittled the wood shaft, carved notches in the arrows, and finished fashioning a bow with pretty good tension. When Badang prepared to leave, I asked about arrows, and he pointed to the knife and a few small trees and told me to make my own. He stressed that I should make the tips as sharp as possible and use only the straightest branches to ensure the accuracy of my shots. Now, in addition to my small hikes, foraging, and rereading my math book, I had a new project to occupy my time. I went to work finding good straight sticks, and with the knife and a rock, I sharpened the arrow tips. Then I found a few pieces of soft rotted fruit and wood and began target practicing. Within a few weeks I became a pretty good shot and downed small birds that I carefully plucked, gutted, and roasted. In addition to providing an extra source of protein, my bow and arrow provided many hours of diversion as I honed my shooting skill and whittled straight and sharp shafts. By no means did I become as accurate as the natives I'd seen using their homemade bows and arrows, but I got a kick out of improving my skill. Archery provided hours of enjoyment and escape from sitting around with nothing to do but feel nervous or sorry about my precarious situation.

Whenever Pio or Badang visited, I would ask for news or even rumors of American, Allied, or Japanese activities in the area. Usually there was no good news and only rumors. I wondered at times if we had lost the entire war and if my hiding would end in my eventual capture. Some days and nights when I heard movements in the thick underbrush or thought I heard voices, I imagined the worst. Increasingly, despite trying to remain calm, I got throbbing headaches during the minutes and hours I felt danger might be nearby. I had survived confrontations with dangerous snakes, spiders, pesky leeches, and other critters, but I worried most about what would happen if the Japs suddenly discovered my hiding place. I also worried about the fate of my friends Badang, Pio, and their families if a spy revealed their role in helping me. I had seen so many awful things over the months, I sincerely hoped God would safely guide Badang and Pio and provide me safety during my isolation.

One rainy morning Badang came to my lean-to and asked me to follow him quickly. I knew he wouldn't ask me to come out of the mountains if it wasn't safe, so I followed. He was a little jittery as we spent an hour hustling down to his house. There I saw his family, and he told me his wife was about to give birth and needed my help since she was having some trouble. He also smiled and said he wanted me to share the joy of their new child. She was already in labor, and I had no earthly idea how I could help in her delivery process. I had never helped or even witnessed a child being born and was embarrassed that Badang expected I might know something about doctoring. I asked Badang what I could do, and he told me to hold her hand and give her comfort so she would relax. I squeezed her hand and gently stroked her arms as Pio and other family members entered the place and huddled with his children to watch. The grown-ups were mumbling prayers, which seemed a blend of Catholicism and their native religion. Within a few minutes, Mary groaned and the baby literally popped out. A woman gathered up the baby, cut the cord, raised up the newborn, and gave it a few shakes, and the new baby bawled. Everyone smiled, Mary gave me a little wink, and a chorus of hallelujahs filled the hut. The older folks and kids patted me on the back and head as though I was some kind of magic man even though my role was minor at best. It was an incredible scene. Pio's wife used a towel to clean up Mary, and one of the kids scooped up the afterbirth and threw it outside. I looked and saw two scraggly mutts gobble it up while furiously wagging their tails. Soon the baby girl was nursing at her mama's breast, and Badang announced the name for the new child would be Marry. I blushed when he announced his new baby was honored and blessed by my presence. Amid the children clapping and adults laughing, I felt a joy I hadn't experienced since being stateside. Here amid all the crap of war, I sensed and shared their feelings of renewal, hope, and family. I was mighty glad Badang had invited me to be a part of this event and now felt a stronger bond with him and his family. Finally, Badang grabbed my hand and vigorously shook it, saying, "Thank you, Mr. Charlie, sir, for your help." This made me feel mighty good, and I damn near busted out in joyful weeping. I hoped with the Lord's help that I might someday share a newborn with my darling Catherine. Within an hour or so, Mary was up and getting together a feast, tidying up the hut while pampering her new child.

After a good, home-cooked meal, I left late in the afternoon with Badang guiding me back up the slopes to my hideout. Three or four days passed without seeing him or Pio, and I wondered if everything was all right down in their barrio. Finally, one day Badang brought good news. He told me the Japanese garrison near his village was moving. This was the first good report I had heard in over a year since Tom was captured and I was pretty much left on my own. The next week Pio greeted me with a broad smile and reported that the Japs had moved away. I felt a burden lifted but stayed at my hut because Badang and I knew there were still informers and sympathizers in the barrio. Not too long after the first good news, more good information arrived. A runner informed Pio that the Japs were moving their troops out of Apayao and Kalinga Provinces. He also said there were stories of a band of friendly guerrillas nearby. This meant

I might end my solitude and rejoin an American insurgent unit. By this time, I estimated that I had probably lost thirty or forty pounds and looked forward to the possibility of quinine, American chow, a good shave, and some clean clothes. Badang brought news that two guerrilla leaders were in the area and specifically searching for Filipino and Americans who were hiding from the Japs. Their names were Captain Swick and Colonel Blackburn.

A few days before they were due to arrive, Badang and I had a long conversation. He thanked me for telling him about America. He loved stories of our modern trains, cars, cities, Hollywood stars, cowboys, my family and Kakie. He never tired of listening and my telling reminded me of home. Badang always emphasized his admiration and loyalty to the faraway country of his dreams. He also mentioned he would probably never leave the islands but hoped his children might have a chance to travel after the Allies beat the Japanese. Obviously, I thanked him and Pio for all their help. I understood, and Badang knew, that he and Pio and their families had saved my life. Finally, as best I can remember, he said, "Now, Mr. Charlie, I hope you will not forget me when you get back to America. As you know, we are poor, simple people, and perhaps you can send us medicine, clothes, tools, a gun, and other things." He added, "You know I was scared the whole time we kept you hidden and we shared our food, but I knew it was the right thing to do." I promised him when I got home I would write and do my best to send him the things he requested. Within a few days of this conversation, I left his village and would never see him again but never forgot his vital assistance.

Matias Badang and family

Pio Paned and barrio councilors

VIII

Headhunters - More Guerrilla Activity

Leaving my hiding place, I continued to feel grateful to Badang and his friends for their help. Without their aid I'm certain I would have been recaptured or died somewhere alone in the wilderness. More than the food and supplies, Badang and Pio offered companionship and conversation during my lonely months. As previously mentioned, the Nips offered rewards to villagers and put pressure on them and their families to turn in military and civilians they considered their enemies. According to Badang, the Japs ransacked their homes, stole their food, confiscated their animals, and took advantage of their girls and women on a regular basis. It was a tricky proposition because one day you might trust a Filipino, and the next day he might turn you in to the enemy. Lakewood was a great example of someone Tom and I totally trusted, but it became increasingly possible he betrayed our location or was forced to reveal our whereabouts. Many of the natives I met, including Badang and Pio, were defenseless and poor and certainly could have used bounty money for medicine and food. I felt extremely lucky that these two brave men never betrayed my trust. Also, I continued to believe God's good graces helped me survive my long period of hiding, waiting for good news, and misadventures.

Word of the Japs pulling out of Apayao Province was great and a godsend for the local people. I certainly hoped MacArthur would return, as he promised, and we could finally whip the enemy and send them away. I knew Doug McArthur was a good and honest man, but my time in the Philippines had been a terrible mess. I think our military leaders didn't do such a hot job in the early weeks of the war. I'm convinced we could have won at Bataan and avoided the death march and other horrible stuff if we had just gotten more supplies and reinforcements. Joining up with Captain Swick and Colonel Blackburn was a good turn of events. It was heartening to once again be with Americans, Filipinos, and other friendly forces in a guerrilla outfit. Even though many of us looked like bums, I trusted we would shortly get boots, clothes, gear, some medical attention, and decent food. Those of us who came out of hiding soon began to look more like soldiers when we got shaved and washed with real soap. It took me a few days, but I finally got a pair of decent used shoes. I had spent the last year running around barefoot and wearing shoes seemed a little strange the first few days. Hiking over rocky and slippery trails made footwear a necessity as we prepared to set off for our new base of operations.

Swick and Blackburn were experienced guerrilla leaders and military officers. After the fall of Bataan, Blackburn escaped the Japs and fled into the jungles and mountains with a few buddies, much like Tom, Red, Steve, and I had done in our run from captivity. Hooking up with other groups of escapees and friendly locals, Blackburn put together teams of men to spy on and harass the Japs. He had been in the Philippines long enough to know many local leaders, the terrain, and the customs of the people. He and his band were constantly on the move evading and harassing the Japs. The enemy placed a reward for his capture dead or alive. I learned Blackburn skillfully used his network of tribal and barrio chiefs, in addition to American civilians, to avoid capture, and he was always a few steps ahead of their pursuers. I later learned Blackburn, the career soldier, had defied the odds to become a major leader in the guerrilla resistance movement. While a few stories floated around about Blackburn having a bad side, regarding his treatment of local women and insisting on the best in rations and housing, he was nonetheless a skilled commander. Captain Swick, on the other hand, was less uppity about his rank and had earned his captain's bars working his way up from the rank of private. Though he was a college man, Swick always seemed friendlier and more respectful to everyone he encountered than Blackburn did. Swick also endured the death march and imprisonment before escaping from the Japanese.

Soon Blackburn and Swick explained our mission to seek higher ground and reinforce a small and remote guerrilla post already in operation. Our exact destination was not disclosed for security reasons. Since the enemy was slowly retreating from their more isolated posts, it would be our job to track and report their movements to the big wigs in Australia. From intelligence reports, our officers reported that the Japs appeared to be moving their forces from the smaller barrios to larger towns and population areas. It seemed they were giving up their isolated positions to consolidate their forces. Since our numbers were always smaller than the Jap forces, we were ordered to resist direct confrontations unless we had no other choice. We were often reminded that our weapons and supplies of ammo and combat gear were much less than our enemy's, so our situation could only be defensive.

As we began our journey to the new base, I encountered others who had also eluded the Japs by hiding with, and in some cases without, help from friendly villagers. Everyone had stories similar to mine, but some were in worse shape than I was. A few guys were very ill, and two or three men acted a little crazy. Of course, we traded details of our hiding, and I asked everyone if they had heard anything about Tommy Pasquel or Lakewood. Nobody knew a damn thing, but Captain Swick did tell me he understood the Japanese were sending healthier prisoners to Japan to perform jobs vacated by Nips forced into military service. This revelation gave me hope that Tom had escaped execution or a second imprisonment, but I continued to think my buddy was probably up in heaven. I enjoyed envisioning Tom getting past Saint Peter at the pearly gates and enjoying a paradise of big juicy steaks, Canadian Club, and curvy Betty Grable honeys. God knows he deserved the best for all the hell he had endured. One day a lieutenant told me the Japs still executed escaped POWs. Further, he explained the Japs' strict warrior code called hara-kiri, which forced many of them to commit suicide rather than surrender or allow themselves to be captured. They thought it was dishonorable for any soldier to give up, and this was the reason they shot escaped POWs. Another officer repeated his belief that Japan desperately needed men to fill vacant jobs as laborers, miners, and dock and factory workers and was transporting many prisoners to fill those jobs. Given the conflicting stories, I just didn't know my buddy's fate for sure but hoped for the best.

As we began our march, I met a young man named Elliot, from Georgia, who was a couple of years younger than me. He had a good sense of humor and a long, country drawl that was entertaining and somewhat akin to the southern talk back home. Like many of us, he had spent months hidden in the mountains and was also helped by people living in a nearby barrio. Ironically, in our conversations we estimated we were never more than ten kilometers apart. We shared the thought about how good it would have been to meet and share some time together. But we agreed it was probably best we never encountered each other because our safety required strict seclusion and never moving far from our hideouts. In the coming days, we became friends and talked about our war experiences, which were identical. Of course, we also reminisced about the good times back home and our loved ones. We both acknowledged our gratitude for encountering the brave Filipinos who helped us and maintained great loyalty to Americans, despite pressure and the ever-present danger of the Nips. Neither of us knew any current news about the war, except what Blackburn and Swick had disclosed. Except when news came from an officer, most of the circulated stories we got were guesses and tidbits of truth mixed with a lot of bullshit. Some of the nutty stories circulating ranged from MacArthur becoming president to General Eisenhower preparing a massive invasion of the Philippines. We had no newspapers or radios, but from what we heard, it seemed the war in the Philippines might be slowly turning in our favor. We also encountered a nice fellow, Bill Carroll from Philadelphia, and others who had also escaped and survived recapture from the Japs.

After a few days' march along twisting foot paths and through heavy brush, we moved into the barrio of Conner. It was a good-sized town that the Japs had abandoned a few weeks earlier. Villagers loyal to the Allies were rounding up suspected traitors and Jap sympathizers for trials and execution. Our movement was slow because a few boys were using makeshift crutches, and the sickest were carried on bamboo pole and canvas litter rigs. Prolonged hunger and the effects of malaria, beriberi, dysentery, and other sicknesses had rendered many men incapable of standing or walking. The sickest men were left in Conner to get better care, rest, or at least a chance to die peacefully. Upon our arrival there, the local folks were in a celebratory mood and gave us a wingding of a party. The villagers were happy to see American and Filipino troops despite our shabby appearance. Looking back, I wonder if their party was for us or an expression of their relief and joy that the Japanese had finally moved away. Anyway, we got healthy portions of freshly cooked meats, fish, fruits, rice, and vegetables. Shooting the breeze with Elliot and others in our group, we reaffirmed our belief that the Filipinos were fine people and certainly favored Americans over the Japanese. After chowing down, we were all ladled a few cups of rice wine, and some in our group got sloppy drunk. A handful jumped up and boogied with the local ladies, but most jabbered with each other or the local folks. Needless to say, it was our first feast in a long while, and everybody had a gay old time.

We spent a few more uneventful days in Conner while more Americans and other Allied soldiers felt safe enough to quit their hiding places. While there we got better clothes, boots, razors, machetes, supplies, and rifles. The clothes were a great improvement over the rags we had been wearing, but I think some of the guns we got were World War I leftovers but nonetheless welcome. The razor blades, soap, and combs did the job in improving our grimy appearance. The joke of the day became anyone cutting himself shaving would not qualify for a Purple Heart medal. In a few hours, we got freshened up and looked and smelled better. Finally, our officers called us together and announced our ultimate destination was a place called Kabugao, which was about twenty miles farther up the mountains in the Kalinga and Apayao areas of Luzon. It would be another tiring uphill trek, but at least our stay in Conner had gotten us well fed and freshened up enough to lift our spirits for the hike.

As usual, the heat and humidity started early in the day and kept us sweaty till sunset or the passing of a cooling rain shower. Our procession often kicked up clouds of dust, and this settled on our exposed skin and, with our perspiration, formed a wet, brown film that wasn't an entirely bad thing. Though it looked nasty, the brown crust prevented more bugs and mosquitoes from biting. We moved quietly and slowly and were ordered to observe silence and muffle our clanging mess kits. Spotters and runners moved ahead and to the flanks of our formation to scout any enemy presence and welcome more hidden comrades into our formation. As we proceeded, we heard no gunfire and knew our advance men were doing a good job helping us avoid enemy troops. A few times we left the established trails and sloshed through creeks and dense forests to avoid the Jap patrols our spotters suspected were nearby. When we stopped to rest, officers told us that at our new post, we would get special training and more gear to track and disrupt Japanese activities and round up traitors and enemy prisoners. The march took four or five days, and as we got closer to the guerrilla base, Elliot and I began noticing guard positions along the ridges. After a few more hours of uphill climbing, we finally reached the base. It had been a tough haul, especially for the sicker men among us.

The new camp was set on a fairly flat stretch of land tucked among the mountains and bordered by stands of palms and other trees. Scattered among the trees were tents, wooden shacks, and lean-to shelters. We encountered and were welcomed by Filipino soldiers, scouts, Americans, and civilians already manning the base. I observed a hundred or so men working and moving around the compound when we arrived. Blackburn immediately ordered his new group to gather. Directed to sit he began to detail our mission and promised to introduce us to the key men staffing the base. As we sat around, he revealed that some of our ships and submarines were just off the coast, and a few of our aircraft had been spotted probably scouting the surrounding area. He indicated while the Japs were clearly still in control, he was sure MacArthur would soon invade the islands. He repeated and emphasized that our primary job was to support Allied efforts with intelligence. He pointed to a tent with antennas and told us the camp had several radio telephone rigs that were capable of communicating with Australia and our offshore ships. Blackburn went on to say the new men, physically able, would be placed into small squads and be given cranky phones and a runner or two to keep in touch with his command post. I was impressed with Blackburn's air of confidence and authority, and his specific plan of action. Elliot and I shared our enthusiasm to once again have meaningful jobs in fighting the Japs and no longer spend our days in hiding.

Elliot and I teamed up and built a little shelter composed of old scraps of canvas, tin, poles, and ropes. The floor of our hut was dirt, and we gathered and used dry grass to make sleeping places on which to spread out our newly issued blankets. We had no mosquito netting and were told to only smoke or make campfires when directed by an officer. In addition to raising smoke signals to the enemy, we were advised wildfires in the surrounding fields of dry grass were a major concern. Meals and coffee came from a mess tent and were available most hours since patrols were coming and going at different times of the day and night. The food was a mix of local tubers, rice, and vegetables with meat or fish sourced from natives or guys in the camp who hunted, fished, or set snares and traps. Once in a while, pineapples, mangoes, and coconut were available. These items were always welcome treats. Our coffee was a brown concoction, and the tobacco issued was a bitter blend but also welcome after many months of skimpy and questionable provisions. After a few days of getting set up and meeting others, an officer called Elliot and I to his tent for a meeting. First, he wanted to know our military rank. Elliot told him he was a second lieutenant, which I didn't know, and I told him I had received a field promotion to buck sergeant. Since Bataan surrendered, very few men wore stripes or officer pins and rarely introduced themselves using their rank. Except for commanders like Blackburn, Swick, and Folksom, most everybody else was just another soldier, and the distinction between privates and officers wasn't considered a big deal. This officer then explained and, to some extent, repeated Blackburn's instructions. He told us to team up with one or two runners, and we would be issued maps, a cranky phone, and specific areas to patrol. Elliot and I had already operated as guerrillas before being forced to hide and knew some of the routine.

We began our new assignment and usually spent a day or two in the field calling in anything we felt might be helpful. Some nights we'd get back to our hut, and other nights we'd shelter in the field or bed down in a friendly village. One of our problems became the efficiency of our cranky phone, and we discovered faulty units were a pretty common occurrence. Not surprisingly, we found several men set up in a hut doing nothing but fixing and piecing together these phones. When our phones went dead, we used runners to report suspected enemy movements or evidence of their abandoned campsites. In addition to gathering intelligence on Japs, we also handled reports of locals who had been spies or sympathized with the enemy. Since the Japs had retreated from some of the barrios, more and more local chiefs and people began to seek revenge on those they considered turncoats. Blackburn had specifically told us our camp had no means to shelter prisoners, and we would be the judge, jury, and executioner in cases involving traitors or captured Japs. The only exception involved English-speaking or high-ranking Jap officers or civilians. These special prisoners had to be hauled before Blackburn or one of his officers for questioning. Since the Sexto Felliciano incident of torture before execution, I was nervous about disposing of Filipinos and relieved that Elliot made the call on those condemned to execution. Sometimes I felt one villager calling out someone as a spy or traitor might simply be part of a long-standing family feud within a barrio. While I hated turncoats as much as anyone else, experience taught me the Japs often made threats against families, which forced some to become unwilling rats. Although I understood and sympathized with some of this, I knew the Americans who were captured or killed because of spies or traitors deserved justice.

I clearly remember one horrible incident involving Colonel Blackburn and two captured turncoats. I found the manner in which the colonel handled this situation was wrong. In my opinion, Blackburn's cruelty was terrible and an ungodly act. One day, two captured natives were hauled into camp, and these men were found guilty of betraying Americans. At Blackburn's direction, their feet and arms were tied, and rags were stuffed in their mouths. He called an assembly and announced these two traitors had disclosed the hiding place of several Americans. These American soldiers were then ambushed, tortured, and eventually killed by the Japs. Using a bullhorn, Blackburn commanded everyone to gather around closely to see how he handled turncoats. At this formation, there were as many Filipino runners and soldiers present as Allied soldiers. Maybe Blackburn's purpose was to scare the assembled Filipinos from messing around with the Japs or becoming their informers. At any rate, he told two native guards to tie the prisoners to posts. At this juncture, I thought Blackburn would simply have the men shot, but a firing squad didn't happen. Instead he directed a beating of the captured men with bamboo sticks. For ten or fifteen minutes, the men were beaten severely on the arms, legs, face, and body. The thick bamboo poles splintered, and when they were ordered to stop, the torturers were clearly out of breath. The terrible beating caused big black-and-blue welts to pop up all over the condemned men's arms and legs. Thick streams of blood began running down their battered bodies. The traitors were breathless and wheezing, and their faces twisted in pain. Next Blackburn ordered the torturers to use sticks to bash their heads. The sounds reminded me of the sharp, cracking noise made when someone squarely hits a baseball with a Louisville slugger. After this treatment, the bound men were nearly unconscious. Their eyes were glazed and wildly rolling. Blood was now oozing out of their ears, eye sockets, and noses, and a bloody foam began dribbling from their mouths. Elliot and I, along with others, looked away; it was sickening. I was standing near Colonel Blackburn and got his attention. I whispered, "Sir, this is torture. For God's sake, why don't we just shoot the bastards?" He looked at me, frowned, and pushed me aside.

Blackburn told the torturers to use their bolos to finish the job. First they were told to whack off their ears and stuff them into their mouths. Then the severed ears were forced down their throats. By this time the prisoners were clearly choking. Finally, Blackburn gave a command in Filipino and made a thumbs-down signal to the guards doing the torturing. At this point, the men raised their bolos and chopped at each side of the men's necks. The cuts were deep, and I was surprised their heads didn't immediately fall off. Their heads violently pitched forward, and blood squirted out of their jugular veins. Then a hard whack was delivered to the back of the men's necks, and this chop sent their heads tumbling to the ground. By now I was sick at my stomach and shocked by what I'd witnessed. As the two traitors hung there headless with their bodies jerking in their final seconds, an old native man rushed up with a wooden bowl and caught their blood, which was squirting out like water from a garden hose. Blackburn grinned as the old guy, stained with red, rushed away, clutching his bowl of fresh blood and cackling.

I was boiling mad and, without thinking, shouted at Blackburn, "Dammit, sir, this is absolutely wrong; the traitors deserved to die but not in this way." Blackburn grabbed me roughly by the shoulders and shouted in my face, "Let me tell you something, son. We're in the Orient, and you know as well as I that the only thing these people understand is torture." He added in a slightly lower voice, "Look, Charlie, we've been through a lot, and we know these damn Asians don't respect human life like we do, and sometimes we have to do things to show our superiority." I shrunk away, hating and fearing the man who was my commander. While Blackburn was a good leader in many ways, I found this disgraceful action unforgivable and totally unnecessary. It was one of the most horrible things I had ever seen. Later, when things calmed down, Elliot and others in our group agreed the traitors deserved execution but not the savage torture Blackburn had ordered.

I still harbor bad memories about this spectacle, and it's something I will never forget. Thankfully, after this gruesome public execution, I don't remember any more shows of such torture ordered by Blackburn or any other officer. Maybe Blackburn felt he delivered a onetime display necessary for the Filipinos watching, or maybe he became concerned that Americans and other Allied soldiers might someday report his brutality. Finally, I never really believed the bunk about Asians treating life as less important than Westerners did.

A day or two later, I was ordered to report to a Lieutenant Johnson and guessed Blackburn was busting me back to private for speaking out against him. I really didn't give a damn about being busted and was surprised when all I got was an ass chewing for what the lieutenant called "disrespecting" a superior officer. He told me I would not be demoted and actually gave me an additional runner and said I might get another field promotion if I could steer clear of criticizing officers and continue to do a good job. He repeated my orders to track and report enemy activities or capture Jap and Filipino traitors. Fortunately, Elliot was with me during my patrols and made the critical call on wasting a Jap soldier or Filipino turncoat. Our Filipino scouts spoke some English and were reliable, but the runners were local men and boys with little military training and not much discipline. Some were schoolboys in their early teens, and sometimes they acted as if we were involved in a game. On one mission we got a tip that a man named Lakewood was hiding in a nearby barrio. He was the son of a bitch who abandoned us and likely told the Nips where Tom and I were hiding. He got Tom captured and probably killed. We slipped in one night and caught the bastard. We tied him up and scooted back into the jungle. I called Blackburn about Lakewood and what he had done. He asked me to make certain it was the same guy. I assured him he was, and the colonel ordered me to go ahead and bury him as soon as possible. I agreed but told Blackburn I wasn't going to torture the guy even though I hated his guts. Blackburn said he didn't give a damn as long as we disposed of him.

I told Lakewood he was going to be executed for being a traitor. At first he was stone-faced, and then he blubbered like a baby. He told me his family and children needed a father, and he was so sorry for what he had done. I listened but reminded him that Tom also had a family, and he should have considered our lives and families before disclosing our location. I told him we treated him like a brother, trusted him, and shared whatever food we had. As far as I was concerned, he became a low-down scoundrel. Elliot was back at camp, so I told two scouts to take Lakewood out in the jungle, make him dig his own grave, kill him, and plant his ass in the ground. I also told them not to torture Lakewood unless they wanted punishment for disobeying my orders. A few hours later, my men returned and said the job was done. I did not regret ordering Lakewood's execution and was relieved Tom's traitor met the fate he deserved. Days later I found out my scouts, despite my orders, had beheaded Lakewood. Since beheading meant instant death, I didn't consider it torture and didn't discipline my men. Among some Filipino tribes, an enemy's head was considered a trophy. My scouts probably got high praise and possibly the pleasure of a village girl for presenting Lakewood's head to a local barrio chief. Sometimes I found it difficult to discipline my Filipino scouts and runners. They carried an incredible amount of hate for the Japanese, and to some extent, based on the suffering they and their families suffered, I understood their rage. All in all, the native men in my squad were usually hardworking and loyal. Sometimes I learned to just look the other way and not ask too many questions when some of their actions broke the rules.

For the most part, we had a lot of success tracking Jap movements and dealing with spies. Once in a while, we got a little too frisky and had to run like hell when we found ourselves outnumbered or accidentally got too close to enemy patrols. More than once we scrambled into the jungles with bullets whizzing all over the place. My squad was fortunate, and none of us ever got shot, but we did suffer numerous cuts and bruises from running headlong into thorns and underbrush. Unfortunately, a few men in other squads got shot and even killed in the course of patrols conducted from our guerrilla base. A little clearing a few hundred feet from our camp was where we buried our casualties. Their graves were marked with bamboo crosses. A written record along with their dog tags, if they had any, was maintained to identify the graves and report their deaths to our commanders in Australia. It was Blackburn's job to collect their personal information and belongings, which eventually got to the families by way of the War Department in Washington. Communication and record keeping were sparse, and to the best of my knowledge, my official status, as reported to Catherine, was missing in action the entire time I was in the Philippines after the fall of Bataan. I learned later that many of us were also reported as AWOL after the death march, which seemed a crazy classification since all semblance of military order and organization fell apart after Bataan.

It was good news when Blackburn told us our reports were directing Allied bombers and fighters to hit enemy locations. He told us this was the first time in a few years that our flyboys were back in the fight to win back the islands. This was great because it proved our tromping around the hills and jungles was a worthwhile mission. Each day we could see and hear a few more American planes overhead and hear the thuds of bombs as they hit Jap locations. When we began to get more ammo and supplies from airdrops, Captain Swick told us to engage the Nips if we thought we could knock down a few. While we continued to quietly sneak around the jungles and woods, we began to catch a few Jap patrols dumb enough to use the well-trodden trails. We continued to harass Jap patrols and got to calling ourselves the "hit-and-run boys." One evening, Swick reminded us our tactics were similar to those used during the Revolutionary War against the superior forces of England. Blackburn and Swick had trained us well to silently move around, pop out of the shadows, knock off a few Japs, and then disappear back into the jungle. I was pleased and a little proud to have moved from being a Jap prisoner and slave to being a soldier again. Captain Swick ordered us to always knock off the trench mortar guy and anybody with an automatic weapon and then blast the hell out of everybody else. He told us we could loot the killed soldiers for any food, gear, supplies, ammo, or weapons, but to leave their personal stuff alone. I respected and understood this, but some of my scouts and runners swiped watches, wallets, rings, and coins off the dead Japs. Again, I refrained from disciplining my scouts and runners unless they wanted to desecrate the dead Nips. Whenever I saw a killed Jap, I remembered the unarmed Americans and Filipinos on the death march who were bayoneted because they simply fell down or became too weak to walk. I felt the men we shot or killed were armed combat soldiers and would have killed us if we hadn't gotten to them first.

Several of our patrols took us close to Conner, and this is where I got my most severe attack of malaria. I had continued to lose weight, but I figured it was from running around so much. But, when I started feeling weak and my temperature shot up to 103 or 104 degrees, I knew something was seriously wrong. At this point, Captain Swick had me sent to Conner. While there was no hospital, medicine, or doctors there, Conner was a fairly safe place for the sick and wounded to get care and rest. Several army medics and local people used local remedies, jerry-rigged splints, crutches, and bandages made from boiled rags to care for the sick and wounded. I remember being drowsy and placed on a cot as my body got hot as fire, and I could barely stand or walk. Hours on end it felt like a blowtorch was cooking my body. Then, at other times, I felt like I was freezing even though they piled blanket upon blanket over me. The burning sensation and frigid feelings would come and go without warning. I also experienced severe headaches where my head felt as if it was about to explode. During this major malaria attack, I also experienced periods when I got numb, shaky, and weak and couldn't lift my arm or leg. I evidently had awful dreams because the medics told me I screamed like a wild man and woke up drenching wet. At the Conner sick bay, they didn't have regular medicine for malaria but concocted a local remedy that sometimes helped. It was a quinine substitute made from prevarian tree bark. The bark was boiled down to a concentrated liquid, and a few teaspoons provided some relief from the terrible symptoms. However, nobody seemed to know the exact strength of the stuff after the bark was cooked. Too strong a mixture made your eyes dilate and got you all woozy and unsteady. Too small a dosage wouldn't help much, and you'd still feel lousy.

Once I got over this major hit of malaria, other health issues soon popped up. Going to the bathroom, I started noticing little wiggling worms. The white suckers were about an inch in length. At first a few worms appeared, then more and more. I was told this was a hookworm infection, and it left me weak and stripped of energy. Again, local remedies were the only ways to treat this medical problem. Some things worked, and other remedies were terrible and, I think, made things worse. For diarrhea and dysentery, we found that taking a few grains of gunpowder from a 30-caliber shell, which contained gentian violet, was a helpful temporary remedy but not a cure. For severe constipation, one fellow came up with a crude way to get things moving. He took a short section of hollowed-out bamboo and attached a little bag made of animal skin or rubber to one end and filled it with water. He'd gently shove the other end of the bamboo stick up his rectum, and as the water slowly squeezed out, it helped flush things and relieve impacted bowels. This homemade enema was one surefire way to help a man stay regular and relieve severe constipation. This procedure worked fine for me several times. Despite our efforts with tropical ailments, malaria and severe dysentery killed many or knocked the hell out of those who survived.

After a few weeks at Conner, I got well and strong enough to resume my work. But at some point, our camp evidently got overly aggressive with our assaults, and the Japs got hopping mad and gathered together a larger force to push hard against Conner and our guerrilla base. When Conner fell back under Japanese control, we were forced to quickly abandon our camp. We then hightailed it forty or so miles deeper into the mountains and ended up in Kalinga Province

near its capital of Apayao. This location gave us a more isolated spot to monitor enemy activities and defend ourselves.
It was also a better location because the Nips had to pass
through several American-fortified and friendly barrios, and
their runners kept us informed. From this new location, we
resumed our patrols and skirmishes. Climbing through thick
jungles, uphill and downhill, and slashing paths with machetes became increasingly rough. As always, the air was
forever thick with humidity or dust, and without shade the
heat made me feel as if I was sitting in a boiling pot. Like
others I had good days and those when I was too sick or
exhausted to do much of anything. In one successful raid,
some of our boys captured Japanese radio gear. With this
better equipment, our radio guys were able to improve communications with MacArthur's headquarters, and Blackburn
told us we were getting more helpful and detailed information from our commanders. They were requesting more data
about Jap troop locations, movements, officers, and enemy
armor and aircraft. We intensified our efforts using our con-
tacts, snitches, runners, and friendly natives to find out every
speck of information. According to Johnson, Swick, and
other officers, our reports and the intelligence from other
guerrilla outfits were proving helpful to MacArthur's staff in
mapping out a return invasion plan.

About this time, and to my great surprise, Blackburn promoted me to lieutenant. It was an acting rank and meant
Blackburn and Swick recognized I was doing a decent job.
Despite this promotion, I still couldn't stand Blackburn because of his use of torture. I followed and respected his orders
because he was the boss. At our new location, Blackburn had
an unusually large hut constructed for his personal use. He

didn't share it with any other officers, and he kept Filipino waiters, maids, and what looked like hookers hanging around all the time. Also, he seemed to get the best food because he used runners to haul in special things from nearby villages in the valley. While realizing commanding officers got special treatment, it seemed enlisted men and officers were living in modest shacks and sharing simple food. While nobody was starving, it seemed to many of us that Blackburn's high life-style just wasn't right when everyone else lived like peons. One captain I knew said he had been with Blackburn a long time, and he had always been a "selfish prick."

Not far from our new camp, native workers began clearing an area that was going to be an airstrip. Swick explained it would provide a place to transport high-ranking, captured Japanese officers to Australia, evacuate our wounded and sick men to ships off the coast, and provide transportation for Blackburn and other officers. One day I detoured my patrol to get a closer look at the place that was going to be a runaway. It looked like a tough job because tall stands of bamboo and heavy vegetation required the workers to flatten the space without the use of any mechanized equipment. Also, they were clearing things without using fires, which would easily give the enemy our exact location. About the same time the airstrip was under construction, Blackburn got word of an American plane shot down nearby and the capture of its pilot. According to his information, the torpedo plane was downed in Aparri, a seacoast village in Cagayan Province about fifty miles north of our encampment. Australian headquarters ordered Blackburn to rescue the pilot, and he immediately organized and sent out a search party. This was a risky mission for the search party since it was a long distance and probably passed through Japanese-held territory. My buddy, Elliot, was chosen. He requested me to come along, but Captain Swick told him my stamina was questionable for such an extended hike. Surprisingly, in about two weeks, the patrol got back with the pilot. Elliot later told me the story of the rescue:

"When we reached the coordinates, we had received from Australia, we found nothing. However, we quietly scouted the area, listening for anything. On the second or third day, a runner came back and told us he found the wreck a mile or so closer to the coast. As we got near the crash site, we saw five Japs and one officer guarding the plane and the pilot tied to a tree. Our plan was to lay low and wait for a chance to ambush the Japs and get our pilot. After many hours hunkered down in the dirt and weeds, a chance finally occurred late one afternoon. All the guards and the officer had gathered around a little fire where they were eating and talking. It was the first time all day we saw them distanced from the plane and prisoner. On a signal, we blasted them with mortars and automatics and rushed in to get our man. All hell broke loose in our surprise attack. The Jap guards and officer scrambled for their weapons, but our gunfire quickly knocked a few down and sent several others running away. They were unable to immediately return fire. We got the pilot untied and then ran like crazy. The whole thing happened in just five or ten minutes, and we carried and half dragged the pilot away as quickly as possible before the Japs could come after us. We knew more Japs would be alerted and soon be in hot pursuit, so we double-timed our departure. It was tough going for a while since our pilot was hobbling slowly due to his busted leg. Finally, a few hours later, we stopped and put together a splint and crutch to help our navy buddy move on his own. Even with our crudely fashioned leg brace, it was slow going. Luckily we encountered no Japs coming or going and got him and ourselves back in one piece."

Everyone was excited and happy our patrol had accomplished its mission. I cannot remember the pilot's name, but Blackburn and the other officers treated him like a king. He got to be friends with the officers and enlisted guys. He was a genuinely nice fellow. He shared a lot of fresh news and verified or squashed some recent rumors. He told us the Allies were pushing the Japs out of New Guinea and moving in our direction. MacArthur was planning to send a huge force to liberate the Philippines. He added that the war in Europe was still rough sledding, but the Allies were finally kicking the hell out of Hitler and the Nazis. However, he added, the bad news was the Japanese were fighting to the last man, and all over the Pacific they were killing civilians and war prisoners while destroying their villages and towns. He mentioned a woman named Tokyo Rose who was broadcasting good music and propaganda every night to GIs all over the Pacific. Later, when we got more radio equipment, we tuned in to enjoy her sultry voice and good American tunes and to laugh at all the crap she was preaching.

After a few weeks, the pilot was getting around well enough to travel, and we found out the US Navy, unlike the army, was going to rescue their man. They were sending a submarine to get him out of the Philippines. Before he left, he told us he would never forget his rescue and the way he had been taken care of. When he got to flying again, he said he would try to locate our camp, do a flyover, and drop us a few goodies. He said if we spotted a low-flying aircraft tipping its wings a few times and throwing out a hat, it would probably be him. We thanked him, but nobody expected anything. However, a few weeks later, we learned from our radio man that a small boat got him off the coast, and he was picked up by a waiting sub. Several months later, and to everyone's surprise, a fighter zoomed down out of a deep- blue sky and tipped its wings several times. The Corsair rushed down toward our new airstrip, circled twice, and dropped several duffel bags, which floated down on little parachutes. After dropping the bags, the speedy plane circled the airfield a few more times and shot away into the clouds. Instantly, we all realized this was our navy buddy the camp had rescued. The bags contained a few Aussie newspapers, cigarettes, small bars of soap, pieces of wrapped candy, a handful of girlie magazines, razors, and a few pouches addressed to Blackburn. Everybody got a little something out of the goody bags. The newspapers and magazines were passed around so much, the print eventually rubbed off. The navy pilot kept his promise, and it was the closest thing to Christmas we had experienced in a long time. Also, the stuff reminded me of the good things I had often enjoyed and perhaps taken for granted back home.

As time moved on, we continued our forays along trails, collecting local turncoats and engaging small Jap patrols still stupid enough to use established trails. Elliot and I, using the best evidence we could gather from local people, continued to be judge, jury, and executioner for spies. It was nasty business and often left me feeling a little depressed. Once or twice we had to take guilty men out of their homes while their wives and children were crying and screaming for mercy. We always tried to contact an officer about our spies, and Blackburn and the other officers consistently ordered us to bury them once we were confident of their guilt. One time we entered a barrio and found several men hung because they had been American informants. Also, we were advised their wives had been raped, tortured, and, along with their children, killed. It was all gruesome business, but to the best of my knowledge, we never went out of our way to physically harm the families of treasonous men. I continued to have days when I had energy and other days when I was too sick to leave the camp and perform my normal duties.

One morning a fellow came into our camp riding a little pony. He was a Filipino Jesuit priest and operated as an old-fashioned, circuit-riding preacher. There were plenty of missionaries of different religions around but not too many circuit riders. He spent a few days with us, and it gave me an opportunity to attend masses and give my confession. After babbling on about the things that bothered me, the Jesuit assured me I was simply doing my job as a soldier and should know that God understood the unusual circumstances of our conflict. We talked several more times, and I ended up feeling a lot better about my situation.

Small, cub-sized Piper airplanes began to take off and land from our little runway on a regular basis. The army planes bounced up and down the dusty, rooted runway but never crashed or flipped over. The pilots were young guys evidently skilled in handling their craft on the rough airstrip and around the nearby mountains. Fuel was still a scarce commodity, so I think most of the flights were sparingly launched to transport officers, important documents, or men seriously injured or sick. I learned that Blackburn, Swick, and the other higher-ranking officers and important civilians used the planes. Sadly, Blackburn reported to us one day that Captain Swick and several of his men had been ambushed while on patrol. The captain was seriously wounded and moved to Lingayen for better medical care. He was the finest officer I encountered during my time as a guerrilla.

It was near the end of 1944, and I had been in the Philippines over three years.

Medical Evacuation

It was late in 1944 when General MacArthur landed in Leyte with a sizable force. Despite my earlier negative impressions of the general, it was good news. At long last, he finally made good on his pledge to return. Furthermore, we were told in addition to the army, our navy and air corps were going gangbusters on the Japs all over the Philippines. However, there was still plenty of enemy activity, as well as horror stories about the Nips massacring prisoners of war and innocent civilians. Enemy patrols continued to operate everywhere, and reports indicated their offensive strategy shifted to a greater emphasis on revenge. While the Allies were gradually winning back the islands, many stories were circulating about the Nips killing Filipinos and committing hara-kiri rather than accepting surrender. Our guerrilla base began getting more and better supplies, in addition to a larger number of Filipino and American reinforcements. Although our camp was still a primitive setup, it was better than living alone in the jungle or at some of the earlier guerrilla hideouts. With fresh reinforcements, better gear, and food,

I was confident we would shortly win back the Philippines and kick out the Japs.

In December, I got busted back to sergeant by a Blackburn order, but I heard he got reduced a few ranks too. I still didn't care whether I was a private, corporal, sergeant, or lieutenant. My major concern was getting home to Catherine in one piece. Later I heard Blackburn's demotion may have occurred because an army big shot found out about his tactics of torture and unsavory treatment of the natives, especially the women. Even though I never liked the guy, he was one tough son of a bitch and a good guerrilla leader. I continued to keep busy with my runners, informants, and scouts patrolling the nearby trails and villages. We were now hauling in a greater number of Jap prisoners, including a few officers who willingly surrendered. Also, more traitors and collaborators were captured, and new orders allowed us to turn these devils over to local barrio leaders and counselors for their trials and disposal.

I continued to get more miserable headaches along with attacks of malaria. In addition to beriberi and other conditions, the frequency of fever, diarrhea, chills, and shakes increased. The nasty white worms also returned in my stool, as well as occasional infestations of lice and fleas in my scalp. Fever blisters and puffy eyes became constant annoyances along with everything else. Despite being in country for a long time, the bugs, leeches, and mosquitoes never gave me a break. I never escaped the pesky things except when I was completely in the water, and then I had to watch out for leeches. Our camp now had supplies of quinine and other medicines, but sometimes the stuff didn't relieve my symptoms or headaches. I wondered if some of my illnesses were beyond relief from the available pills and potions and if my future would be filled with medical difficulties. One episode of sickness kept me flat on my back for over a week, and despite better food I just couldn't put much meat back on my bones.

I remember an odd encounter about this time in an isolated barrio we entered. As usual we first reported to the chief, which was regular procedure, and like many natives the old man spoke no English. No one in his lodge spoke English, and my runners were unfamiliar with the words they spoke. The old man was flanked by several husky, bolo-toting younger tribesmen. Their allegiance to Americans or Japs was questionable since a small flag of each nation was hanging prominently in the hut. This display worried me, but I assumed these guys felt both flags would keep them safe from the Japs and the Allies. Several times the old boy gestured at us aggressively and barked orders to the younger men. All along he maintained a scowling stare at our group. Although we were armed, I wasn't sure what might happen next. I sensed any gesture of aggression on our part might cause his young tribe members to attack us with their bolos. As my anxiety grew, I thought how we might gracefully exit this hut and get the hell away from this angry old man and his henchmen.

Then, out of nowhere, a teenage boy appeared and spoke enough English to translate. The boy told me his chief was a legendary headhunter and more interested in adding our heads to his collection than anything else. The young man communicated our greetings and peaceful mission to the old man, but his unfriendly grimace remained fixed. The boy said the old fellow and his tribe had a special hut that contained the shrunken heads of men from other tribes and even some foreigners. After a few more nervous minutes, I decided a gift might free us from this uncomfortable confrontation, so I dug into my pocket and pulled out a few crumpled peso notes. I gave the old man a polite bow and offered the money. His face slowly twisted into a toothless smile, and he returned my bow while accepting the money. I bowed back again and motioned my squad to slowly exit the hut.

The old chief jumped to his feet, blocked the doorway, and bid us to follow him. With our young translator following and insisting it was okay, we were led to a small thatched hut. The interior was dark, smelly, and dimly lit by candles. Thin bamboo staffs topped with tiny shrunken heads stuck on top were posted everywhere. The aged chief smiled and happily jabbered as our translator told us we were getting a tour and stories of his battle trophies. It was an interesting yet scary tour looking at several dozen bronze-colored human heads shrunk to the size of softballs. Each was adorned with normal length facial and head hair. After a half hour of his bragging, we all exchanged more bows and exited his shrine. The boy followed us for a while and told me the gift of money may have saved us from something "very bad." This was my last encounter with any headhunters, and although the grisly practice had been officially outlawed by the Philippine government for years, it continued in isolated parts of the country. Whenever I met up with tribes involved in this primitive ritual, I always experienced mixed feelings of fear and curiosity.

I was delighted to see more American planes flying over-head and began to feel more confident we'd win this damn war. I gained a sense of hopeful anticipation as I realized our pushback of the Japs meant my ticket back home might not be too far off. Because of my experience living off the land, an officer recommended, and Blackburn approved, me as a trainer for new men joining our group. These relief troops were local Filipino volunteers and American soldiers fresh from Australia. I felt this was a good assignment because it gave me a chance to share what I knew from my own ex-periences and things Badang and other natives had taught me. Also, it gave my body a good break from hiking hills and trampling through jungles while running patrols. I ex-plained to our fresh troops everything I knew about avoiding the Japs and surviving in the jungle, as well as guerrilla tac-tics, native customs, seasonal weather, dangerous animals, survival foods, and enemy tactics. I also knew the new guys represented my replacement, and this motivated me to help them understand all I had experienced and learned. My stu-dents brought fresh news, much of it good, from the world outside the Philippines. Their reliable reports debunked the Tokyo Rose propaganda, enemy leaflets, and crazy rumors, which for too long served as my only sources of information. For four years, my world had shrunk so much, and every-thing they related gave me little glimpses into the times I had missed. As always, every night I thought of Catherine, home, and my family, and this kept my spirits up but some-times left me a little blue. Our long separation, lack of mail, and the time we missed being together bothered the hell out of me. I guessed folks back home had no earthly idea of my status. The war Department regularly sent Catherine post-cards reminding her of my uncertain status.

Because of my weight loss, lousy health, and diminished physical stamina, the officers finally relieved me of all patrol and camp duties. I was allowed to just hang around the base, instruct the new men, and piddle with fixing equipment. Some days just getting up and walking left me dizzy, and I quickly became tired. Also, there were days when I had no appetite and other times when the simplest foods caused my stomach to churn and hurt. When the chills and fevers got really bad, I was confined to my cot. Other fellas at the guerrilla base were also in rough shape. Some spent their days bedridden in medic tents. Whenever I got to feeling lousy and sorry for myself, I thought about the men who were sicker than me. It seemed every week a few more men died and were buried in a nearby graveyard with white wooden markers bearing their names.

It was rumored and then confirmed that the sickest among us would be evacuated by flights from our small airstrip. The destination was Lingayen Gulf on the west coast, where a shipping port had been established and was securely held by the Allies. I learned from a pilot, who frequently flew down to Lingayen, the port also had a large medical facility for medical evacuees and hospital ships poised to ship the sick back to the states. Simply marching to Lingayen from Kabugao was not possible because the Japs still held large portions of the countryside, and most of us were too weak for such a hike. Although an occasional doctor visited our base, most of our care came from medics and Filipino nurses and helpers. With the limited amount of medicines available, they did their best to render medical assistance.

Since my duties were light, I had time and an opportunity to meet a few local people. Nearby there was a Catholic mission and school, where I met Father Omer and Rev. Joseph Poot, along with teachers Prisca and George Dinagtuan. I found good counsel and interesting discussions with them. Prisca and George were excited about the upcoming birth of their first child. They believed and hoped their baby would come into a new world of peace and enjoy a good life, and they said a boy baby would be a great blessing. I remember enjoying talks about naming their new baby. They reassured and teased me that someday I would also have children and experience the joy of a new life. I sometimes found this a far-off hope but knew having children was a dream Catherine and I had shared before the war. My conversations and confessions with the priests centered around the guilt and sorrow I had experienced. I was constantly troubled that so many guys, just like me, were tortured and killed, and I was helpless to change their fate. I also worried a lot about Tom and whether there was something I could have done to prevent his capture. I frankly felt a little guilt over the fact I had survived while seeing so many others perish. While I thanked the Lord and felt fortunate to survive, I questioned and couldn't understand how God allowed so much misery and suffering. These concerns and others were always popping up in my thoughts, dreams, and discussions with the priests and the Dinagtuans. They helped me cope with my feelings of grief and anxiety, and to slowly understand that my survival was a great gift from the Lord and left me responsible to lead a good and honest life. I was guided by these good people, and although my body was sick, my spirit and conscience became refreshed at their mission and school. Inspired by the joy Prisca and George shared with the new life in their family, I decided Kakie and I would definitely have children someday, and if a baby boy came into our lives, he would be named after my faithful buddy, Tommy Pasquel. The Dinagtuans and priests teased me that God would ultimately decide the gender and Catherine deserved a say in naming our children. Despite our long separation and without communication over the past few years, I never doubted Catherine had been faithful to our marriage vows.

These new acquaintances were different from Matias Badang, Pio Pinad, and other natives who kept me safely sheltered in the mountains and helped me survive. These folks were well educated and interested in the world beyond their villages and the Philippines. They were not rich but had more material things than the people I had encountered in the isolated hamlets and barrios. While Badang and his neighbors struggled for food and survival, these new friends were middle class. Father Omer had been stationed in China before the war and shared many interesting stories about his experiences. Father and I often prayed and talked and it was a healthy experience. Our friendship and discussions helped me replace some of my sadness with hope for a better future.

I met others too since we used local folks around our base for different jobs. I especially remember the Rodriguez sisters because they were bright and cheerful young ladies who desperately wanted to leave their homeland for the United States. Many Filipinos shared their dream, but the Rodriguez girls constantly asked how and when they could immigrate. By all accounts and based on my observations, they were good young ladies and not whores, but they seemed willing to marry any GI if it could get them to the states. Of course, with a war going on, nobody was going anywhere. I believe when the war ended, many Filipino women did use marriage as a means to leave the islands and sometimes brought along their parents, grandparents, and other relatives. I never found out if the Rodriguez sisters' dream was fulfilled.

Our little airstrip in Repong was near Conner, and I began to see more and more small planes coming and going every day. This was an encouraging sign, and my hopes of evacuation increased. One of our camp officers revealed to me their plan to fly me to the gulf once the sicker soldiers were rescued. He told me Lingayen had many doctors, good medicine, and medical facilities. However, he cautioned me to be patient since combat-wounded and gravely ill men were first priority. I understood this but was nonetheless happy to realize better medicine and deliverance from the war was soon coming. One morning, to my great surprise, Blackburn appeared at my bedside, and with an uncharacteristic smile, he presented me with a brown envelope. He told me I had been a good soldier and my day of evacuation had at last arrived. He wished me well and shook my hand.

During my service with guerrilla outfits, I served with the 11th and 14th Infantries under the command of Officers Swick, Blackburn, Nobles, Frank, Moses, and several others.

The hike to Repong was only a mile, and I stumbled over every root and loose stone along the path until a younger man helped me reach the airstrip. They hoisted me and strapped me into the passenger seat, which was directly behind the pilot's seat. The plane was an L5, which was a two-seat, single-engine, open-cockpit observation plane. It was a small aircraft roughly the size of a civilian Piper cub and carried no guns. Once belted into place, the pilot turned my way, smiled, and gave me a thumbs-up. He hollered that I should hold on as he revved up the engine. As I recall, the pilot's name was Bill, and he wore shiny silver lieutenant bars. As we rumbled down the grassy field, he looked back and shouted, "Hold on, sir." I had never flown before, so I was a little apprehensive but happy to be heading out of the jungle. The L5 backfired a few times as we raced down the runway, and just when I thought the plane might explode or crash, it slowly lifted off the ground. The motor was spitting puffs of gray and white smoke, and I tasted oil spraying from the engine. The first seconds airborne felt like someone had pulled a giant rug from under me, and I soon experienced a feeling of nausea, but it passed as the cool air replaced the gassy fumes.

When I was a little kid, I remember watching airplanes and thinking it was a kind of magic seeing the big machines buzzing around the sky like giant birds. I had absolutely no idea how airplanes actually worked but was happy to be moving quickly to a secure location. Soon, the shaking eased and the engine got quieter. It was a weird sensation, and still feeling a little nervous, I looked down. I remember thinking this ride was as scary and exciting as the dips and speed of the Ocean View roller coasters I had ridden years earlier. Finally, I felt secure and somewhat relaxed, and I was amused the pilot had earlier called me "sir" as if I was an officer or old man. While I may have been a year or two older than the pilot, it seemed weird to be called sir. Soon I enjoyed viewing the jungle below. It was all so beautiful. The trails and creeks looked like brown and blue ribbons, and the terraced rice paddies and garden plots appeared like colorful squares in my granny's quilt. The mountains were covered with a soft green blanket, and the villages, carts, and people along the roads appeared as small toy-sized objects. I was surprised by all the natural beauty I could see in a place where so much daily horror and destruction were occurring. It was weird to realize the pain and suffering of war in a place that looked very much like a tropical paradise. Despite a rough takeoff, we leveled off and the ride became smooth. Wispy morning fog and clouds were still clinging to the hills and sliding by like smoke. In my briefing I was told that after my flight to Lingayen Gulf, I would be medically evaluated and then placed on a navy ship for transport back to the states. I guessed I'd be home in a month or two and reveled in the prospect as we gently moved along.

Then, out of nowhere, a deafening blast of sound and strong wind shook our little plane, and it bounced and violently dropped. Bill screamed something, but I couldn't hear a damn thing. Looking forward, I saw the reason for his alarm and our sudden change in stability. A single fighter plane had just blasted by us, and its fuselage bore the distinct red ball of a Jap fighter. It was in fact a Jap zero obviously hot on our trail, and I instantly realized our slow speed and lack of guns made us a sitting duck. There didn't appear to be anywhere we could safely land among the hills and forests, and I thought it was a heck of a note that after four years surviving on the ground, I might get blown out of the sky the day of my evacuation. I strained to look and noticed the zero making a big U-turn and heading back our way. By this time, Bill was twisting, zigzagging, and diving our small plane every which way, trying to keep us from being an easy target.

I clenched, prayed, and almost peed my pants expecting the worst as our craft jerked around the sky. By the time the zero turned and began to close in for another strafing run, the pilot had dropped us down to tree level, and just as I tensed up and thought we were goners, a real miracle happened. The zero abruptly veered off its deadly course and blasted straight up into the clouds. Within a few seconds we saw and heard the reason the zero dramatically quit its deadly attack. To our rear, two tiny dots in the distance instantly grew larger and turned into a pair of speedy P-38s. They shot past us, which again caused us to bump around, and chased after the Jap zero. It was an unbelievable moment to see the stars and bars on those wings as they whizzed by in pursuit of the enemy fighter. All this probably transpired in a few seconds or minutes, but I swear it felt like hours. Leveling back into a smoother flight pattern, Bill turned around and flashed a huge, reassuring grin. I smiled back but tasted a few salty drops of fear dribbling down my face. I spent the next few minutes thanking God and thinking how lucky we had been to escape and remain airborne.

Our journey continued uneventfully for another half hour as I slowly got comfortable again, knowing we would soon reach our destination. Then Bill dropped the plane down low and reduced its speed. At first I thought this meant we were about to land, but all I could see below were hills and forests and certainly no runway. He then shouted back something like "Sir, I've lost my bearings, so relax and be patient while I figure this out." I thought, "Hell's bells, this kid is lost." I shouted back and asked if the compass was working, and he hunched his shoulders, which I took to mean he wasn't sure. Having a general idea of Philippine geography, I shouted to simply head in a westerly direction until we reached the South China Sea. I knew once we reached the water, we could land on a beach and get directions on how to reach Lingayen. He sheepishly nodded back while giving his compass a few thumps. Since it was a clear day, I was confident this would work and hoped our plane wouldn't run out of fuel. As a prisoner, I had been in the Lingayen Gulf area and knew once we reached the coast, the naval base would either be north or south along the west coast.

We flew on, and the horizon of deep green forests and hills slowly gave way to marshes, beaches, and the sea. At last I knew we were on the right track, and he then turned left, which meant a southerly course. We flew over the coast and coastal road, and Bill turned and asked me how much farther. I yelled back I had no earthly idea. I told him we should land on the beach and ask a local for directions. I thought this had become a crazy ride with a pilot who wasn't quite sure which way to go. I found out later his radio and compass were malfunctioning, and this made things difficult. I guess this is what the old expression "flying by the seat of your pants" meant. We slid over the coast, and looking down, there were large brown smudges every few miles. I soon realized these were little villages burned to the ground. I suspected the enemy had pillaged and then destroyed these coastal barrios as they retreated. Some of the places were still smoking, and I told Bill to land between the burned-out barrios, and hopefully someone would be around to give us directions. He nodded and, within a few minutes, landed on a sandy stretch a few feet from gently lapping waves. After a few minutes, two half-naked Filipino boys rushed to the plane. They laughed, stroked, and hugged the plane while trying to climb aboard. Behind them, a man arrived smiling and greeted us with bows and a few English words. Above the noise of the idling engine, the pilot asked about the Lingayen base. The man pointed south and used his hands to indicate it was a short distance. We thanked him and stretched out to shake his hand. The pilot handed over a few cans of rations and a half bagful of candy to the guy, and the boys snatched the candy and danced like crazy over the sweets. I handed the native the only thing I had: a half pack of Lucky Strikes. Bill then shooed the boys away and powered the motor, and we sped down the hard sand and lifted skyward. I looked back, and the men and boys were still smiling and wildly waving. Within about thirty minutes, the gray naval ships of the port came into view, and after a few circles of the runway, we made a smooth landing.

I was happy and relieved the trip was over, especially since it was far from a routine flight. Bill climbed out of the cockpit and came around to me and apologized for the rough ride during our encounter with the zero. Obviously, he had no control over our near-fatal encounter or his equipment, so I thanked him and assured him he did a great job. We talked for a few minutes and shared a smoke, and he told me after dozens of similar flights, he had never been attacked by an enemy fighter or dealt with so much messed-up equipment. As he and an orderly pulled me out of my seat, we shook hands, and my young pilot flashed a final broad smile and said, "Good luck, sir." While I was thrilled to have my feet back on solid ground again, I ended up a nervous wreck from my first-ever airplane ride and a little irritated being called sir.

Supported by an orderly, an ambulance rolled up, and a hospital helper grabbed my envelope and duffel bag. He helped me ease onto a stretcher and then loaded me with another soldier aboard his ambulance. We sped away, and I was delivered to a giant canvas tent. Soon a doctor and nurse began looking over my papers and filling out forms lickety-split. The doc looked me straight in the eye and asked how I was feeling. As I mumbled my complaints, he nodded and scribbled away. After a nurse took my temperature and felt my pulse, the doctor returned and said, "Sergeant Joyner, we're going to get you some good medicine and chow and then get you on board a ship to go home." After my eventful flight, I was exhausted and whispered a thank-you. Within a few hours, they drew blood, gave me a few shots, and had me swallow a handful of pills. I lost track of time and fell asleep, but I later woke up feeling quite relaxed and smelling pretty good. Evidently, while I snoozed, someone had stripped me of my nasty clothes and given me a bath. I was now dressed in clean underwear and pajamas.

For the next few days, I got hourly doses of medicine along with small meals, snacks, and cups of juice. One day an army doctor came along and asked me to tell him about my childhood, mother, father, feelings, and a lot of other goofy stuff. I patiently answered all his questions but finally told him I wasn't a nut ball. He reassured me his questions were standard procedure, and he didn't think I was a nut. Later, a fellow in a nearby bed told me the guy was something called a shrink. Soon, when I felt stronger, they allowed me out of bed and escorted me to a patient lounge. I was assigned an orderly, and his job was to accompany me and help me get around. The lounge was a nice setup of comfortable chairs, sofas, card tables, pretty nurses, and a refreshment stand serving coffee, Coca-Cola, smokes, popcorn, and candy. I nibbled a few things that my mind told me would be good, but my stomach didn't like too much. The best place I discovered was a small desk stacked with postcards and writing paper. I immediately wrote Catherine a postcard to tell her I was all right, safe, and would soon be heading home. It was a short message, and I saw no need to add a lot of details since I knew this would worry her. I knew there would be time to share my experiences once I got back to Portsmouth.

I encountered some men in the lounge who had been freed from POW camps and others who had been wounded in recent fighting. Several guys had stories very similar to mine, but nobody, including me, wanted to talk much about our experiences. Mostly the talk was about getting out of the Philippines and back home to the regular world. I enjoyed hearing about wives, sweethearts, children, families, big steaks, real American milk, good cigarettes, and all the other good things we had missed and would soon experience again. I noticed a few men who rarely spoke and knew they suffered from shell shock, or what some called battle fatigue. The lounge was a wonderful place. Reading current newspapers and magazines, I learned we had finally whipped Hitler and had the Japs retreating all over the Pacific. Our orderlies were more like waiters and would light cigarettes and bring snacks or drinks if you simply asked. One afternoon I discovered the lounge had a telegraph station, and I fired off a short message to Catherine repeating what I had written in the postcard. I knew the telegram would get to her quicker than the postcard. It was a good feeling to inform my darling wife and family that I was alive, kicking, and homeward bound. Unbeknownst to me, Catherine saved the telegram and pasted it in a scrapbook. Months later, I read and recalled my short message: "Honey, I'm OK and heading home. Your loving husband, Dinky." While it was short and sweet, it surely lifted her years of waiting and worrying over my long isolation and missing-in-action status.

After a few days, I was feeling and sleeping better and also suffering fewer headaches. Even though I still got winded and a little dizzy on my feet, I began asking the doctors and nurses when I could get aboard one of the ships. Early on the fourth day, a doctor came by and shuffled through the thick file of my medical records, flashed a frown, and told me he was kicking me out of the place. I was puzzled at first since I was feeling a lot better and didn't understand his scowl. Then he chuckled and winked. "Son, good luck and Godspeed, you're going home." With this, the doctor handed me my thick file and shook my hand. Boy, did this report make me feel good since I knew I would shortly be heading home. In quick order an orderly arrived with a wheelchair and my full duffel bag of stuff. He said, "Okay, Sarge, I'm going to help you get ready for the ship." Out of the duffel, he pulled a set of brand-new fatigues, underwear, shoes, socks, and a cap. I hadn't seen brand-new clothes since my first duty station at Clark. The fresh smell and feel of the items were a welcome change from the scruffy outfits I had been wearing for months on end. He helped me get dressed and seated in the wheelchair. He plopped the duffel and my records in my lap and told me to hold on tight. As I left, a few men cheered my departure from their beds, and I shouted back that I hoped they would soon be headed home too. We moved quickly toward the ship, and looking back, I realized the large hospital tent I had been in was only one of dozens. Soon we fell into a procession of wheelchairs, stretchers, and men walking toward a huge gray vessel. It wasn't a warship, and from my experience at the navy yard, it looked more like a transport or cargo carrier. I noticed several antiaircraft guns mounted on the decks but saw no large guns. At the ramp we moved slowly up to the ship's main deck, and my orderly patted my back as a navy man steered me on board. I looked around at the other men, and even though I was skinny, a lot of them were skinnier, and some looked to be in worse shape than me. However, it was a great moment, and many guys already aboard were smoking, smiling, and joking with each other and the ship's crew. Just before stepping on board, a navy officer greeted each passenger with a sharp salute and a hearty "Welcome aboard, sir."

Once aboard I was allowed to walk and was escorted down a few decks to get assigned a cot and locker. This bay contained many cots, a few canvas hammocks, gurneys, and large hospital beds. I met a few other men, and the general atmosphere of excitement brightened the dull gray paint and cold steel of our new dormitory. Medics, doctors, and nurses were rushing around, checking on the bedridden and asking everybody else how they were feeling. I questioned one medic about the ship, and he told me it was a transport vessel that had been rigged up as a floating hospital. I learned later that surgeries and other medical procedures were done on the wounded and seriously ill men. Since we weren't allowed to smoke below the main deck, many of us made our way up a few ladders to the daylight. I asked one other crewman about our journey, and he said it was his understanding that we would first steam to New Guinea, pick up more evacuees, and then set sail for San Francisco. This sounded mighty good to me, and he added he thought the trip would take a few weeks if all went well. His "if all went well" comment stuck in my head as a warning. But I dismissed it as meaning if fair weather prevailed and the ship had no mechanical problems. As I encountered other evacuees, I asked if anyone knew of my pal Tommy Pasquel, but nobody did. When I recounted his capture to one marine, he told me he had heard that many men recaptured by the Japs, who were fit, were shipped off to Japan in what they called "hell ships" to perform jobs vacated by the many Japs called to military service. Tom was in pretty good physical shape the last time we were together, so I hoped he ended up in Japan and was surviving whatever work assignment he'd been given.

I found a shaded spot topside with several others and watched and listened as preparations were made to cast off. Crewmen and officers were busy shouting orders back and forth, and then the ship's horn blared several times. As we slowly pushed away from the dock, large clouds of smoke filled the sky, which indicated the ship's engines were cranking into action. With seagulls and other sea birds squawking and diving around the dock and ship, I watched the harbor and surrounding countryside slowly move away. I was glad my service in the Philippines was coming to an end, and my thoughts happily turned to getting back home. I was excited about seeing Catherine again, reconnecting with my old pals and family, and returning to civilian life. Moving away from the mainland, I daydreamed about getting a regular job, saving some money, and getting Kakie Baby and me a place of our own with, perhaps, a houseful of kids and cats.

As the sky darkened on my first night at sea, a million stars popped into view, and I enjoyed the gentle motion of the ship and the breezy taste of fresh salt air. Sipping a mug of joe and smoking a Lucky Strike, I believed the war and danger from the Japanese was at last coming to an end. However, I was wrong.

Hospital Ship - Heading Home

The first few days on board were comfortable. We enjoyed good weather, calm seas, and a navy crew bending over backward to help us feel welcome. The regular chow was good with plenty of extra portions. I noticed some men ate like hogs while others barely nibbled at their meals. I ate some but not too much at one time or any spicy items since my stomach got upset easily. Snack stations were set up all over the ship dispensing coffee, juice, and cookies. The cooks and their helpers treated us like hotel guests and big shots when it came to special food requests or treats when the mess hall was closed. Since most of us came aboard half-starved, the good meats, fruits, and vegetables were helping us regain weight and get stronger. Every day I was dispensed pills or shots, and one doctor told me malaria and some of the other diseases I had contracted might remain in my body a long time. He said the medicines would help control but never completely cure the symptoms, which could come back in the future. Also, I got to see a dentist, and he told me my bleeding gums were caused by something called pyorrhea, and the inflammation might require dental surgery in the future. Despite these less-than-encouraging reports, I was beginning to gain a few pounds and feel better.

In addition to spending the day sitting around topside, there were exercise classes for those who wished to participate. The workouts were simple and never mandatory. I tried some of the stretching and small weight-lifting routines, but I tired easily even though I knew it was an important part of regaining my strength. Most of the time, guys simply sat around the main deck, talked about getting home, or played cards and craps with their leftover pesos and military script. I found magazines on board and enjoyed reading the old issues, which were new news to me. *Stars and Stripes* and other bulletin newssheets revealed a lot of history I had missed when I was deep in the mountains and jungles. I was surprised Joe Stalin had joined up with the US and Britain in getting after Hitler and a little shaken over how old and sick President Roosevelt looked in the newspaper photos. His photos made it obvious our commander in chief suffered the strain of war like many of his soldiers and sailors. My brother Willy was deployed to Europe before I left home, and I sure hoped he got home in one piece. I assumed brother Elwood was still working at the shipyard. I think my sisters had gotten married, and I sure looked forward to seeing them all. I found the stories of the Detroit car companies retooling to build tanks, jeeps, and artillery pieces and the speed of modern shipbuilding fascinating reading.

Although we were supposed to sleep in our assigned bunks, many of us chose to sleep on the wooden decks at night.

With a pillow and light blanket, I found this especially soothing when the seas were calm and the dark skies danced with shimmering stars. Guards on watch roamed the decks at night and gently nudged us to get below but never forced anyone unless the seas rocked the boat. While a few men suffered with sea sickness, most did well since the seas were calm. A count of patients was required each night, and those of us wandering from our cots probably were a pain in the neck for those responsible for verifying rosters. I slept well on those nights, visualizing a happy future with Catherine, kids, our own home, an automobile, and a little vegetable garden. Of course, still being in the tropics, intense heat, humidity, and sudden downpours occasionally chased us from the top deck to the lower decks where big black fans blew the air around.

I remember one afternoon a chief petty officer decked out in his dress uniform came around and told everyone to form ranks and remain at parade rest until ordered otherwise. Nobody understood why. This was the first time in a long time any of us had lined up in a regular military formation. Within a few minutes, a voice over the ship's public address system ordered everyone, not on duty to remove their covers and come to attention. Then a detail of six sailors in dress whites shuffled into sight carrying a body draped in an American flag. Behind them followed several officers in their dress uniforms rigged with their medals and ribbons. The flag-draped body was placed on a plank, and although I was too far away to hear, I think prayers or words were then spoken. Next, over the loud speaker came the sharp and mournful sound of taps at the same moment the body slid down the plank into the ocean. The flag was then neatly folded by regular sailors and handed to an officer. Nobody knew for sure, but we speculated one of our sicker or seriously wounded buddies had passed away. It was a sad and sobering thing, realizing one of our guys had probably toughed his way through the brutal years in the Philippines and was just too sick or torn up to make it all the way home. Things were quiet the rest of the day. Best I can recall, two or three other men were buried at sea during our trip to Frisco.

I asked one crew member how much longer before we hit New Guinea, and he told me a few days. He also mentioned we were part of a naval convoy. He explained that our vessel was one of a group of ships sailing in line, which included several supply and well-armed ships. He further added we were still in enemy waters. This sailor pointed out a thin trail of smoke ahead and astern, and it was the first time I realized we were part of a convoy. I never saw any of the escort ships until we got close to New Guinea. Even though I had worked at the naval shipyard in Portsmouth, I really didn't know a lot about ships and how the navy operated. Based on the good people and food on this boat, I joked with one crewman that if I had a chance to change things, I would have joined the navy.

Except for a few tropical rainstorms storms full of spiky lightning and booming thunder, the passage was generally calm. On the fifth or sixth day at sea, the quiet morning exploded with the ear-splitting sounds of whistles, sirens, and horns. There was mass confusion, and all hell broke loose. A navy fellow began ordering everyone to get off the deck. He was screaming, cussing, and pushing guys toward the hatches and stairwells. One GI with me yelled, "Why the hell we got to get off the deck?" A crewman got right up in his face and said, "Cause there's a goddamned Jap sub inside our convoy." Some navy men were rushing to battle stations and the guns mounted on the deck. I knew this was a bad situation, and despite routine fire, lifeboat, and attack drills we had experienced, this incident seemed serious. Briefly I remembered the old war movies seen as a kid when submarines blew up surface ships, and I wondered the best way to survive the worst if it occurred. The captain began violent steering to the left and right as heavier and darker smoke poured out of the smokestack. I figured the captain was speeding up and twisting the ship to avoid getting hit by a torpedo. In all the mayhem, noise, and greasy smoke showering down, I ran but didn't go below. I found a little concealed spot behind a large gray storage box and hunched down. Two other men were already crouched there, and one of them shouted to me, "I ain't going to go below and get trapped like a damn rat." I felt exactly the same way and thought being topside would at least allow me a chance to jump off the boat and not get drowned under the main deck. After about an hour, the ship stopped zigzagging, and as we slowed down, an "all clear" message was repeated over the public address system several times. Not sure if we were in hot water for not going below, we cautiously moved from our hiding spot and were met by a skinny sailor. He laughed and told us he knew we were hiding the whole time. He added we were jackasses to stay topside but understood some army guys were goofballs. I never found out for sure, but many thought a solitary Jap sub had been detected and chased away or sunk by the war ships in our convoy. All in all, it was a damn good scare, but I still think I would stay topside and take my chances if such a thing happened again. Thankfully, this was my last encounter with the enemy.

By the time our ship anchored at New Guinea, the weather was blazing hot. We didn't have any regular short pants, so a lot of men just wore their underwear or cut off their fatigue pants above the knee. We were a sloppy bunch and some days joked to each other that we looked like a bunch of pirates. The officers, doctors, and nurses were forgiving and never commented on our unmilitary appearance. Orderlies even mixed up lotions to help us avoid blisters and sunburn. We docked in New Guinea about a day while taking on more supplies, fuel, and military passengers. Nobody was allowed to get off the ship, except the navy guys. As we chugged away, a voice over the loudspeaker announced, "Ladies and gentlemen, our next stop will be San Francisco." I remember a deafening cheer filling the air and everybody grinning and joking around. The announcement also reminded me that among our number were many nurses and civilian POW women heading home.

Day by day my appetite got better. One day a doctor reminded me that I weighed only ninety-eight pounds when I was checked in at Lingayen, but now I was weighing in at one ten. As my weight increased, my energy and spirits improved. As we quietly moved over the ocean, my thoughts increasingly turned to getting back to civilian life. Unlike my brother Willy, I had no intention of making the army my career. I felt I had done my duty and never wanted to get too far away from home ever again. I tried to figure out what I would do when I got home. Before the war I had worked at the shipyard, and a counselor on board told me most employers, especially the federal government, guaranteed veterans their old jobs when they returned home. I also found out that the Veterans Administration was offering benefits to finance guys who wanted to go to college or arrange financing to buy a home. Since my grandma yanked me out of high school in the tenth grade, I wasn't too interested in finishing school and realized my best bet was to get a job and make some money. When I left home in forty-one, Catherine was still living with her folks on Lansing Avenue, so finding a home to rent or buy was my number one goal. After the fall of Bataan, nobody got paid, so I realized I was due three years of back pay for the time I was a POW, listed as missing in action, alone in the jungle, and operating as a guerrilla. I had no idea how much money this would amount to but thought it would provide a good start for setting up a household and getting a car.

Every day of the voyage I was getting medicine and doctor or nurse exams, and I was finally beginning to feel my old self coming back. One day another doctor reminded me that my medical problems would linger in my system for a long time, and maintaining my health would require monitoring by civilian or Veterans Administration doctors. Since I was feeling good, I didn't focus much on their warnings but instead felt blessed and a bit lucky to be in better shape than many of the others on board. I remember every night a few men screaming or walking in their sleep, as well as others who constantly mumbled or never spoke to anyone. Along with the others, I spent time talking to and getting to know some of the bedridden guys. I reassured them their health would return and better days were in their future. It was sometimes tough talking about a bright future to a man missing an arm or leg or totally blind. Fortunately, in addition to our efforts, members of the medical staff were constantly at the bedside or nearby the worst-off patients. As I focused more on a bright future, I experienced fewer headaches and bad dreams, and I think this was because hope of better days was replacing the depression and fatigue of constantly being in danger.

I cannot overstate how nice and accommodating the navy crew was to their skinny, injured, and scraggily passengers. At every turn, they seemed to accommodate us with whatever we wanted. I especially remember a fellow waking me late one night and inviting me along with two of his pals to an ice cream party. At first I thought he was crazy, but a big chocolate sundae was something I hadn't tasted in a very long time so I followed. Like naughty schoolkids we tiptoed to the galley, switched on an overhead light, and started rummaging through the freezer and food lockers for goodies. Our quiet foraging was soon interrupted by a commanding voice that demanded, "What the hell are you monkeys up to?" Busted, we sheepishly tried to explain our mischief and were pleasantly surprised when the cook's mate chuckled. He pulled out all the fixings for a proper midnight dessert snack. A few other night owls joined us as we happily consumed ice cream with all the toppings and cookies. Even as a child I cannot remember having so much fun over chunks of ice cream crowned with mounds of chocolate syrup, nuts, and cherries. After an hour of desserts and joking, we finished and offered to help clean up, but the navy fellow would have none of it and told us to get the hell to bed.

Clerks on board handed out forms and brochures with good information about our VA benefits and stuff like that. Further, they explained the procedures and process to file. I began to feel everything would work out if I followed their instructions. In one meeting we were told a thorough checkup and medical evaluation at a hospital was our first assignment when we reached the West Coast. Also, we were advised the Red Cross and government would assist us in getting in touch with our families and arrange getting us home. At about this time, along with others, I was issued a duffel bag of fresh clothes. The kit included everything from new underclothes and shiny dress shoes to a dress uniform decked out with sergeant stripes and a bunch of ribbons. I tried on my new duds and found some of the items hung loosely but laughed with others about our scarecrow appearance in uniforms larger than our bodies. We reassured each other if we put on the "feed bag" overtime until we landed, we'd fill out our new uniforms. The night before our arrival, we were ordered to carefully pack everything in our duffel bags, except for our dress uniforms and shoes. We were also told the bag of clothes and gear given us at Lingayen should be left on board. Finally, word came that we'd get help carrying our duffels off the ship if we wished. It had been a long trip that allowed me to regain some weight and energy, so I decided to carry my own bag. I didn't sleep much the last night aboard because I was excited about getting my feet back on the ground and getting closer to home.

I was on deck when land was spotted, and although it was a hazy and foggy morning, the sight of land looked mighty good. Though the trip was uneventful, except for the Jap submarine scare, I was ready for dry land. We cheered and hooted when a little boat came alongside and used its water cannon to shoot sprays of welcome. In another hour or so, the ship was tied up and the gang plank was lowered. First off were the men on stretchers and in wheelchairs, and I noticed as they descended to the dock a crowd of civilians and military people cheering and waving little flags like crazy. I cannot describe how happy, lucky, and proud I felt as my turn came, and I stepped off the ship and was finally home. I fought back emotions of sadness, thinking about Tom and all my other buddies who would never get this hero's welcome. Even though I was lugging a duffel bag that seemed to be getting heavier with each step, I was floating on air knowing I had survived and would soon be with my Kakie Baby, family, and friends. At the end of the ramp, a cute, smiling Red Cross girl tossed an olive drab green sweater and blanket on my shoulder and shouted, "Welcome home, soldier." Even though it was very nice, the sweater and blanket added a little more weight to my bag. After a few more steps, I saw ambulances and buses awaiting passengers. When I got close to the bus, an army private grabbed my bag and told me to hold on to the sweater and vest and get on board. Once the bus was loaded, the driver turned and shouted, "Welcome home, boys. We're on our way to Letterman General Hospital." It was chilly, and I donned the sweater as we pulled away from the port.

A long-distance operator connected me to brother Elwood, who was with my uncle Joe Culpepper. Boy was it good to hear their voices. Elwood assured me Catherine and everyone else was excited about my return, and Joe said I was reported in the local paper as a hero. Elwood told me he and Martha had a new baby boy, and Willy was heading home from Germany with a war bride named Rita. I also was informed that sisters Mary and Peggy were doing well and had children. I then called Catherine's next-door neighbor, Mr. Frank Burkett, who had the nearest phone to Catherine's home. I nervously waited on the line a few minutes while he rushed to get her. Finally, she answered. At first Kakie bawled like a baby and reassured me she never gave up hope I would make it home. The sound of her sweet voice and crying were moments of joy I'll never forget. We exchanged words, renewing our love for each other. I tried to be cheerful and told her I was okay, just a little skinner, but I knew her mother's good cooking would help me regain my weight. She told me everyone in her family was happy I had survived and looked forward to a joyful reunion. She made a funny comment about the new babies her sisters Frances and Virginia and brother Jimmy had and the fact that our marriages had occurred about the same time. Without thinking much, I responded, "Honey, are you sterile?" It was a stupid thing to say, given our long separation, and I finally promised we would take care of the baby situation the moment I got home. For years, and two children later, she teased me about my dumb "sterile" question. She also was a little peeved I called Elwood first, but frankly after a four-year absence, I needed reassurance that Kakie was okay and still faithfully awaiting my return. Actually, in my heart of hearts, I always knew she would wait, but realizing how long our separation was, I would not have been surprised otherwise.

After ten days of rest, medicine, and head-shrinking sessions at Letterman General Hospital, I finally got my discharge orders. I was given two weeks leave to return home and then had orders to report to McGuire Veterans

Hospital in Richmond. Still thin and wearing a few ugly fever blisters on my lips, I headed for home. The plane rides and landings crossing the country were comfortable compared to my first flight a few months earlier to Lingayen. Stewardesses provided us with plenty of pop, snacks, and good, all-American cigarettes the whole journey. I sat next to a marine from West Virginia who was on his way home too. We talked a lot about our homecomings and very little about our military experiences. When our plane finally landed in Norfolk, I came down the ramp and rushed to Catherine for a very long hug. It was wonderful to suck in the salt air of home blowing off the Chesapeake Bay. We didn't say much for a while. But holding my darling wife tightly and seeing the love in her teary eyes, I realized after nearly four years of waiting and surviving, I was finally home and with the love of my life.

Charles - 1945

Epilogue

When my father returned to Portsmouth, he received front-page coverage in the *Norfolk Ledger-Dispatch*. In its June 1, 1945, edition, a headline proclaimed, "Portsmouth Man Home after Dodging Japs in Philippines for 27 Months." The news account described his "many months of lonely existence in the jungle." It detailed the atrocities he witnessed, the headhunters, primitive living conditions, encounters with dangerous snakes, physical and emotional trauma, escape from a Japanese slave-labor detail, and his role as a guerrilla fighter. The dateline was Richmond since he was, at the time, a patient at Richmond's McGuire Veterans Hospital. In addition to local reporters, he gave several interviews to the Associated Press. More news of his experiences appeared in local newspapers for weeks after his arrival home. Finally, one day he told the reporters he didn't want to tell his stories anymore and just wanted to go fishing. Years later, he confided to me that the retelling caused him to experience an increase in headaches and bad dreams.

During his long absence, and to his surprise, Catherine joined the Women's Army Auxiliary Corps (WAAC). She served honorably and felt it was her contribution to the war effort. Her service surely filled the lonely months waiting for his safe return. Within weeks of getting home, my father happily learned his war buddy, Tom Pasquel, had survived the war. After his capture, the Japanese shipped him from the Philippines to Japan on a hell ship. Until liberation, Tom labored in coal mines and lived under harsh conditions. He endured severe whippings that etched permanent scars on his back. Tom was liberated shortly after the atomic bombs were dropped. My father and Tom had reunions in the early fifties and kept in touch the rest of their lives. In the spring of 1946, true to my father's promise, I was given the middle name Thomas in his honor. Tom and his wife, Fran, were my baptismal godparents. In later years, he retired to Florida and died in 1996. My father also discovered that his escape buddies, Steve and Red, survived the war. Sadly, his guerilla partner, Lieutenant Charles Elliot, did not survive.

His favorite guerrilla commander, Captain G. H. Swick, was promoted to major, survived his combat injuries, and returned home to Arizona. Colonel Donald D. Blackburn continued his army career and became an important figure in the development of US Special Forces. He served during the Korean and Vietnam conflicts, became a general, and was the subject of a 1955 book and 1959 movie. Blackburn returned to Georgia and died in 2008.

As promised, Dad wrote to Matias Badang and Pio Pinad and told them of his safe return. He continued communication with them and their families well into the 1990s. Also, he filled their requests for clothing, patent medicines, and garden tools. In late 1945, Dad received an unusual request from Badang, which read in part, "Because of my intimate relationship with you, I do not hesitate to ask you the favor to buy me a shotgun. If you can buy me one, it will be my remembrance for you, and I will be proud indeed to have a gun because of you." Fulfilling the request took four years and a lot of paperwork, but Badang got his shotgun in 1950. He later called the shotgun "a great gift of friendship from my brother Charlie." Over the years, letters from the Badang, Pinad, , and Dinagtuan families were exchanged. In the mid-1990s, I joined my father in sending letters to the descendants of Badang and Pio until we were told local postal employees often stole money.

Pio Pinad died in 1954, and Matias Badang passed in 1991. Marry, his youngest daughter, reported his treasured shotgun was seized by the New People's Army (NPA), and she said this broke his heart. My father never saw these Filipinos again but always praised their kindness, counsel, and help as critical elements in his survival.

Shortly after his return and honorable discharge from the army, Father returned to civil service at the naval air station in 1945 as an apprentice electrician. He eventually rose to the position of an electronics inspector. He enjoyed and excelled in this job, but he had to retire due to a host of recurring medical problems that required frequent treatments and consultations with VA hospitals and private doctors. In November 1965, at the age of forty-seven, and after twenty-six years of combined federal service, he received a disability retirement. After his retirement he became a private contractor involved in general home repairs, painting, and electrical projects. Later he earned his real estate license. When a friend began manufacturing portable toilets, he provided my father with a pickup and trailer to haul them to locations in the Northeast. The traveling and flexible schedule allowed my mother to accompany him, and he turned this occupation into enjoyable sightseeing opportunities.

Initially, upon his honorable military separation in 1945, he was granted a 30 percent disability rating and a small monthly stipend from the Veterans Administration. Given the extent of his contracted tropical diseases, nervous condition, and dietary deficiencies, he was advised by doctors and decided to seek a greater disability rating. After thousands of pages of communication, congressional letters of assistance, doctors' reports, and VA board reviews, my father finally received 100 percent disability status in 1993. He often joked that this effort was more grueling in some ways than his frightening time in the Philippines. He received the Bronze Star medal in 1985. In the forty-eight years between 1945 and 1993, many issues had to be resolved to establish his military status and disability compensation. Dad and other military personnel who had POW, MIA, and guerrilla status during their service presented new issues for the War Department and later the Department of Defense to resolve. Many official military records from the Philippine campaign were incomplete, lost, or destroyed. After the death march, some captured soldiers and Filipino scouts were listed as AWOL even though they were prisoners of war, escapees, or guerrilla insurgents. Determining the connection between medical problems and military service was a slow process for Washington, Congress, and the Veterans Administration.

Additionally, a major fire at the St. Louis depository of military records in 1973 painfully slowed the process of information collection and verification. These situations required my father and others to seek affidavits from eye witnesses and other survivors to verify their claims. I remember growing up and seeing the constant stream of mail from the VA requesting more information and medical records.

Dad suffered a great deal of disappointment and angst over the negative rulings and never-ending requests for more documentation. However, he never gave up hope, and with his campaign of persistent letter writing, support from his doctors, and the intercession of Virginia and federal lawmakers, he finally achieved his goal.

His medical problems were linked to the extreme conditions of his service in the Philippines. Malaria, beriberi, hookworms, starvation, sinus conditions, gastric disturbances, and chronic nervousness developed during this period. Over the years these medical problems led to heart disease, stomach ulcers, gum disease, diabetes, and cancer. In the mid-1970s, his doctors did not approve his request for open heart surgery. However, by the early eighties, the procedure improved, and he underwent the first of four successful heart surgeries.

I vividly remember accompanying him many times to the Hampton Veterans Hospital for dental operations. Because of his gum disease, all his teeth were removed, parts of his gums cut away, and upper and lower dentures installed. I was too young to drive at the time but accompanied him to lend support. Many times the results of his dental procedures left him numb and in a great deal of pain. I also recall another period when his stomach was so sensitive, he ate only crumbled white bread mushed into milk. This situation was due to stomach ulcers and a lack of normal digestive acids. As a little boy, I heard his screams and groans in the middle of the night when he awoke with nightmares about his terrible wartime experiences. Although he experienced a large number of medical challenges, worries, and recuperation periods, he always maintained a positive attitude. In every instance when I accompanied him to a doctor's visit, his first question to the physician after the consultation or treatment was "So when will I be well enough to go fishing again?"

After securing two or three rentals after returning from the Philippines, my parents' dream for their own home began to take shape in late 1949. For a ten-dollar filing fee, they purchased a 2.1-acre wooded parcel in Norfolk County, now Chesapeake, Virginia. By this time, my sister Catherine Marie was two years old, and I was four. With little cash, he put together our first home with great help from family members and friends. It was a slow process, as his helpers had only weekends available for the construction project, and Dad worked all week at his regular job. Ironically, and following a tight budget, he discovered an unusual building material when he purchased several hundred used wooden ammunition boxes, which became part of the exterior walls. Dad and his coworkers pieced together the house's infrastructure without much help from licensed tradesmen or official approvals from county building officials. With little experience, they built a septic tank and found a good source of well water.

During the early winter of 1950, the house became habitable. Interior finishing and painting were completed months thereafter. I vaguely remember, and am reminded by an early photograph, our home at the time. It resembled a big box sheathed in black tar paper and topped by a shiny tin roof. Nonetheless, it was a warm and comfortable place, and he constantly upgraded it during our dozen years of occupancy. After seventy years, the home stands handsome and sturdy with enhancements to its original primitive look. It was and remains an original creation amid clusters of prefabricated homes that now line Jolliff Road. My father later helped build several other homes, but he was proudest of what we called the "ammo box" house.

My father had many talents. In addition to home-building skills, he had a knack for fixing autos and electrical and plumbing devices. I also marveled at his archery skills. When I was a kid, he used his homemade bow and store-bought arrows to down two squirrels high up in a pine tree one day, and he even nailed a flying squirrel in flight. His quarry became our meal one evening, and thereafter I considered him as legendary a bowman as Robin Hood. He also loved dancing and, with my mother in tow, took lessons to learn all the latest steps. For years he happily displayed his graceful moves at the local Moose Club and nearby Moon Light Room. He took up oil and acrylic painting and produced very delicate and pastoral scenes. In these paintings he centered a deer, pheasant, or other wild animal in flight or motion. Though a predator was never pictured, one could easily imagine the creature escaping some unseen danger. I believe his works reflected his lingering memories of escaping the enemy. He also did a few portraits and used copper wire and tin cans to fashion trees, airplanes, and rocking chairs. After one grueling surgery, he constructed a highly detailed dollhouse for his granddaughter Charmaine and told me later that getting it done was an important step in his recovery.

His favorite avocation was saltwater fishing. From boats offshore Ocean View and Poquoson to the piers and beaches of the Outer Banks, he reveled in the sport. While vacationing at a beach cottage, where many amusements were available, he always chose to fish whether it was sunny or rainy. Not surprisingly, my father consistently caught the greatest number and largest fish at every outing. I think he was a superior fisher because he was patient and perhaps possessed an unusual sensitivity to nature. He also loved to travel and made many trips to visit his daughter and grandsons in Charlotte, and along with brothers and sisters-in-law, he and my mother enjoyed exploring Florida, the Carolinas, and nearby Blue Ridge and Smoky Mountains.

He was a very religious person and never wavered in his beliefs, tithing, or church attendance. Following Catholic Church expectations of the fifties and sixties, he ensured my sister and I received a Catholic education and never allowed us to eat meat on Fridays or any other holy day of obligation. On one occasion he sold a hog, which he had planned to have butchered, to pay a few months of our parochial school tuition. However, to my surprise, he always claimed a back pew at Mass, and I once asked him why. Without hesitation, his response was "Heck, I want to beat the rush." Mother never became a Catholic but was well versed in all the Catholic rules and, along with Dad, kept my sister and me on the straight and narrow. Despite his strong faith, he never argued or discussed religion with any of his Baptist or Lutheran friends or in-laws, with one exception. I vividly recall a local Baptist preacher named Reverend Van Noy, who regularly visited my mother, as a modern-day, car-driving circuit rider. Whenever the reverend encountered my father, they would calmly discuss and then argue and sometimes end up in yelling matches as they compared the merits of their religious beliefs. Fortunately, I never recall fists flying during any of these impassioned conversations.

For over thirty years, and except for an occasional overheard story to an older family member or friend, I rarely heard him discuss his young life and war experiences. He consistently refused to detail his military service to me. As I got older and learned more of the Philippine campaign of World War II, my curiosity about his experiences increased. In 1985, after one of his heart surgeries when he received the Bronze Star, I felt it was a good time to ask again. I requested that he consider detailing his war stories and life as a memoir for family and friends. He agreed. While I knew a lot about my mother's kin, I knew little of his family history and asked him to also include memories of his younger days. I suggested, and he accepted, a tape recorder as an easy way to conveniently relate his stories. I supplied a list of general questions and told him to take his time with the project. I didn't want him to feel any pressure, so no deadline was set to complete the recordings. A few years later, he finished and gave me 266 minutes of recordings and boxes of military records, letters, news clippings, medical reports, and Veterans Administration communications. With so much material, I suggested his life might make a good book or memoir. He was pleased with this and encouraged me to someday take on the project.

After he earned full disability payments, his finances improved greatly, which allowed him an interesting new pursuit. After decades of patching cars and parts together to provide transportation, he finally reached the time when he could afford a brand-new automobile. During the eighties and nineties, he purchased and sold an astounding number and variety of new and slightly used cars and small trucks. Once, when he prepared to trade in a very nice vehicle that was less than a year old for a new model, I questioned his rationale. His response was classic and went something like this: "Well, Tommy, the tires are getting a little worn on this model, and the salesman gave me such a good deal on a brand-new car, I just couldn't refuse." After hearing this and its variations many times, I decided this was his pleasure, and being of sound mind, he should enjoy his car buying, so I no longer questioned his frequent vehicle deals. Another twist to his car purchasing occurred when he bought his first Japanese automobile. When questioned, he replied that, except for the inhumane actions of a few Japanese commanders and soldiers, he never had a problem with the Japanese people. Further, he insisted that since *Consumer Reports* had given favorable reviews to the current Toyota and Honda models over Detroit's cars, he was comfortable and confident with his new choices.

As he celebrated his seventieth and then eightieth birthdays, he seemed amazed by his longevity and relatively good health given so many medical challenges. He began to refer to himself as a tough old bird, a survivor, or a turkey buzzard.

When his weight reached 180 pounds and his hair began to gray, he set about dieting and stocking up on hair-coloring potions. As he aged, he remained on the move and used any excuse to jump into his car and visit the mall or commissary, do household shopping, taxi folks for doctor visits, deliver ladies for their hair appointments, or visit Catherine Marie and her family. For a period of time, he also enjoyed meeting his older brother, Elwood, for a Hardee's breakfast before a day of fishing at Craney Island in Portsmouth.

In 1950, when his brother Willy was killed in action during the Korean conflict, my father began assisting his wife, Rita, and daughter Mary Anita . He provided Rita moral support and assistance with the paperwork necessary for her to get full survivor benefits. He also performed many household repair projects for her. His assistance went on for a good while as she adapted to the culture and ways of her new homeland. As he aged, his generosity increased. In addition to donating to a host of charitable organizations and fulfilling his church pledges, Dad helped younger family members. When they asked or were in a bad way, he provided cash, meals, and shelter. My parents' small home often became a refuge for young moms and playpens full of children. He was never a rich man but always seemed willing to share whatever he had with others who needed a little help.

Another interesting thing was Dad always kept our pantry, refrigerator, and freezer well stocked. Though our food was simple fare, we never missed a meal. I was a fat kid and have spent my entire life pleasingly plump. Interestingly enough, a few years ago while attending a Bataan/POW survivor convention in Norfolk, I discovered a possible reason, or excuse, for my lifetime of portliness. A female psychiatrist who conducted an intensive clinical study wrote a book about a phenomenon that occurred among prisoners of war. Her findings indicated that surviving soldiers who were starved or suffered inadequate nourishment over an extended period of time often overcompensated when they returned to civilian life. Their reactions were evidenced by storing and even hoarding more food than necessary. Interestingly, she revealed these survivors of starvation didn't necessarily overeat themselves, but family members and especially children were provided and even encouraged to eat more food than necessary. I found it an illuminating and informative report. While I would never use it as the reason for my lifetime of pudginess, I wonder if his starving time in the Philippines, years before my birth, affected my body chemistry.

Shortly after September 11, 2001, my father was rushed to Maryview Hospital, suffering from breathing difficulties and severe back pains. Once summoned, I arrived at the emergency room shortly after his admission. As usual he downplayed his distress, but his pain and discomfort were obvious. The ER physician gave him some medicine and a referral to meet with a specialist. I took him to the appointment because by this time he was unable to drive and needed a wheelchair. After an examination the doctor met my father and me in his office. The doctor revealed that Dad had lung cancer, and radiation treatments might be of some value. It was a grim scene, but with his usual optimism, my father meekly asked the doctor if the treatments might allow him to go "fishing in the spring." The doctor didn't answer, and I instantly sensed that my father's spirit sank. Radiation was a wasted procedure and actually became a painful experience. In early 2002,

Dad was placed on oxygen. Since I was still employed and my sister was six hours away, cousins Kathy, Colleen, and Christina volunteered to help. Eventually Christina became his driver and constant companion. Although Mom was available, she was weak and could hardly walk, so strong, young Christina, who could lift my father, became his primary caregiver. Despite his declining health, he still tinkered with gadgets and rigged long air lines throughout the house so the large oxygen tanks could be hidden in closets. He also rigged smaller oxygen tanks onto his wheelchair.

In the winter chill of February 2002, he began calling relatives. He told them about his medical condition and how much he loved them. Later I discovered a few people he called didn't realize he was actually saying goodbye. In his last month of life, he called his parish priest to receive extreme unction two times. I asked him why he felt he needed the sacrament twice, and he related with a grin that he had sometimes been a "very bad boy" and would need extra help to get past Saint Peter. In his final days, he reviewed with me all his last wishes down to the hymns he wanted sung at his funeral service. Finally, in his last days, he accepted morphine to relieve his severe and constant pain. Ironically, morphine had been a rare commodity during his time in the Philippines but was now mercifully available. He died in his sleep on March 11, 2002. Lying beside him in his final hour was his Kakie Baby and Honey. He quietly passed, lying next to his faithful and loving wife of sixty-one years.

He made his last tape recording on December 28, 1988. He titled this piece, "Moments to Remember." In this recording his voice stuttered and brimmed with emotion. I believe his words are a good summary of his war experiences and a tribute to the force he always believed responsible for his survival:

Dawn, the first encounter. The attack, frightened to death, bullets flying, bombs hitting all around, firing at the planes, sweating, can't see how I can ever make it. The death march, twisted, bloated bodies, drinking water where dead bodies lie, no food for nine days, excessive heat, malaria, dead everywhere, over one hundred (degrees). Buddies are dying, barbed wire all around, people trying to help, rejected, carrying out dead daily, the lack of water, food, toilets, completely depressed. Escape, swimming the rapids, being shot at, the trench mortars, up the mountains, sleeping in the pig pens, chased the pigs out, raining, happy, free. Tom's capture, now completely all alone, no weapons, no food, lost, night falls, sleep in piles of leaves piled over me. Wake up in the morning with a wild boar rustling in the leaves, lowest point of my life. Badang's decision, decision was made by natives with Badang's help not to take my head and turn it over to the Japs. They pointed to the jungles where I must go; they were afraid for me to stay in the village for their safety. Thirteen months alone. Day after day I longed for home. I think, I imagine things, I dream, but the days come and go. I came through it all. Don't tell me there is no God.

Marie and Tommy on steps of ammo box house (1950-51)

Catherine and Charles - early 1950's

Author with Godparents Tom and Fran Pasquel

1st Communion Sunday for Charles Thomas

1st Communion Sunday for Catherine Marie

Master Fisherman

"Humble Hero"
Charles R. Joyner 1918 - 2002

CPSIA information can be obtained
at www.ICGtesting.com
Printed in the USA
FFHW020713240119
50280164-55303FF

9 781977 204516